CAPSTONE

smart
business

JAMES LEIBERT

The right of James Leibert to be identified as the author of this work has been asserted in accordance with the Copyright, Designs and Patents Act 1988

First published 2002
Second edition published 2004 by
Capstone Publishing Limited (A Wiley Company)
The Atrium
Southern Gate
Chichester
West Sussex PO19 8SQ
http://www.wileyeurope.com

CIP catalogue records for this book are available from the British Library and the US Library of Congress

ISBN 1-84112-583-0

10 9 8 7 6 5 4 3 2 1

Typeset in 10/14pt Meridien by
Sparks, Oxford, UK
http://www.sparks.co.uk
Printed and bound by
T.J. International Ltd, Padstow, Cornwall

This book is printed on acid-free paper

Substantial discounts on bulk quantities of Capstone books are available to corporations, professional associations and other organizations.

For details telephone John Wiley & Sons on (+44) 1243 770441, fax (+44)1243 770571 or e-mail CorporateDevelopment@wiley.co.uk *for Jane*

Contents

Acknowledgments

I really enjoyed writing this book. I learned more researching and writing it than I could ever have imagined. And I had a lot of fun along the way.

My thanks to all at L.E.K. Consulting, in particular Chris Recny, for allowing me to take an extended sabbatical to write this book.

Thanks to my partner Jane for not getting too upset at having to go to work every day while I 'worked' at home. Thanks for your Herculean efforts helping me edit the completed manuscript and for providing a voice of sanity to counter my wilder ideas. Thanks for all the love and unwavering support you've given me.

Thank you Adam Hall at L.E.K. Jakarta and Kevin Looi at Loudcloud in San Francisco for your enthusiasm and ideas and for your detailed comments. I really appreciated your contributions and they've helped to make this a much better book.

I'm very grateful to Leela Rao and Richard Fuller who, at various times during my career, have given me much needed guidance and to whom I owe much of my personal success in business.

The list of writers, thinkers, friends, co-workers, clients, teachers and fellow advisers who have contributed to my business education and given me inspiration is far too long to list here. But to each and every one of you: thank you.

Finally, thanks to Mark Allin at Capstone for your faith and support during this project. And to John Moseley for nursing the book through to completion.

James Leibert,
Sydney 2002

Summary of Ideas

Businesses aim to create customer value efficiently

- Business allows people to greatly multiply the number of products and services they can create (and receive) in order to meet their needs and wants (Chapter 3).

- The main guiding principle of business is therefore to find ways to meet people's needs efficiently: efficient customer value creation (Chapter 3).

- Customer value creation means:

  - Finding innovative approaches to identifying and meeting customers' needs and wants (Chapter 4).
  - Educating potential customers about the value they can receive from products (Chapters 5/6).

- Efficiency comes about from:

  - Technology investment – a large up-front investment in a new technology that enables lower per-unit costs (Chapter 7).
  - Learning/specialization – learning how to be more efficient and sharing that knowledge (Chapter 8).

- Development of industry-leading competencies that speed innovation and allow competition-beating efficiencies (Chapter 8).

Business strategy is about finding potential opportunities and fending off competitors

- Companies must find good opportunities for value creation by:

  - Understanding and satisfying customers' needs better (Chapter 4).
  - Predicting how market dynamics (trends and product lifecycles) will affect business opportunities (Chapter 11).

- Companies can use the following strategies to fend off competition:

  - Focus on a single customer segment or product position that is easier to defend against competition (Chapter 4).
  - Develop better business processes for systematically improving efficient customer value creation (e.g. customer need identification, product innovation, product development, decision-making ability, learning) (Chapter 12).
  - Dominate limited industry resources (Chapter 12).

- Often alliances with other companies can help to obtain critical industry resources and efficiencies from cooperation (Chapter 12).

Businesses must often be large and complex, requiring good management practices to stay efficient

- Large groups of people need to be divided into smaller, more manageable groups. Tasks/people that are highly inter-dependent should be grouped together to enable greater efficiency (Chapter 14).

- Managers need monitoring systems to get useful information to help them make the right decisions. In particular they need to be able to monitor the company's financial position (Chapter 16).

- Businesses face a constantly changing environment. Managers must make the company adapt to its new business environment. The biggest obstacle faced in making large-scale organizational changes is employee resistance – change programmes therefore focus primarily on overcoming this resistance (Chapter 15).

Management needs are changing in response to new demands

- Management styles have developed over time as the needs of organizations have changed. Management practices that are common today have developed from the need to develop efficiency at a large scale. But business needs are changing.

- Today, businesses need to cope with rapid change and make more effective use of specialized experts. These needs are driving a new management style:

  - Setting broad goals rather than specific duties and procedures (Chapter 10).
  - Empowering employees to make more decisions, become more autonomous and help to lead change (Chapters 10/15).
  - Greater use of small, self-managed teams rather than hierarchical organization structures (Chapter 14).

Achieve personal success in business through honesty and systematic improvement of skills

- The best approach to corporate politics is to focus on the best interests of the company, be open and honest and insist on hard data rather than opinion in decision-making (Chapter 18).

- Personal success in business comes from finding a work environment that suits you, developing critical inter-personal/management skills and applying them to solving challenging problems (Chapters 2/19/20).

Introduction

This is Business

1 Smart Business

The aims of this book

Welcome to *Smart Business*!

It seems an impossible task to cover the whole of business in one short book such as this. Certainly in 300 brief pages we will go on a high-speed tour through the smartest ideas in business. We'll skip from marketing to production to management. We'll take in the grand strategic visions of corporate monoliths, we'll look at the petty tricks of organizational politics and we'll look at what makes for a great entrepreneurial idea. And if we sometimes tread lightly, it's because there is a lot to get through.

I can hear you shouting: 'Jack of all trades, master of none! ... Focus!' This book seems to fly in the face of its own advice to focus on a few key goals. By trying to do so much, surely it risks falling short of everything?

The aim of this book isn't to replace a whole library of business wisdom. You're not going to become a master marketing tactician, or a finance guru, or a great manager just by reading this book. Instead it aims to teach you about one thing, something all the other books miss: business itself. Here's your chance to really see the forest for the trees.

This book provides a holistic view of business, so that you can discern the central themes. Instead of seeing business as a series of conflicting corporate divisions and disciplines, each with its own independent ideas, you will discover how all the functions of business cooperate to achieve a single purpose. When you see how everything fits together, you will become a truly smart business person.

Whether you are an entrepreneur, a junior manager, a sales professional, an engineer, a consultant or simply an interested consumer, then here you can learn about how business works and why it does what it does.

Good luck!

Smart people to have on your side: meet the team

This book features commentary from the 'Smart people to have on your side'. These are some of the most celebrated minds in business. The ideas in this book are largely theirs, so it's interesting to read something about the people behind the ideas. The Smart People listed below have made such a wide-ranging impact that we'll see their ideas throughout this book. We'll also meet other Smart People who have insightful things to say about their own specialities.

Peter Drucker – pioneering and prolific management writer
Management professor at Claremont University, where the business school is now named after him, and at Harvard. A long-time contributor to the *Wall Street Journal*, Peter Drucker practically invented 'management' as a serious academic discipline and has pioneered many of the big ideas in management such as decentralization, customer-focus, competencies, MBO and knowledge work. Drucker has something profound to say on nearly every topic in this book, having contributed more than 30 articles to the *Harvard Business Review* over 50 years and written several important books. Many other manage-

ment thinkers have built their contributions on developments of his ideas. His contribution therefore runs far deeper than his deep but rarely read books.

Adam Smith – pioneering free-market economist
Adam Smith was a professor of Moral Philosophy at Glasgow University. Adam Smith was not really a management thinker, and even worse, his fame rests on a book written over 200 years ago. Yet Adam Smith remains important for his insights into the role of business in the economy and how business achieves efficiency through specialization and competition. These ideas may be old, but they are still relevant to business today.

Tom Peters – investigator of 'excellent' companies and popularizer of management ideas
Peters teamed up with McKinsey colleague Robert Waterman to write the 1980s management bestseller *In Search of Excellence* and changed business overnight. *In Search of Excellence* was the first really popular management book (amongst managers at any rate). It was a call to arms against overly bureaucratic American companies that had 'lost their way'. It exposed managers to the radical ideas taking shape in excellent companies, amongst management thinkers, and in Japan. Peters followed this up with an update that stressed that companies also needed to be excellent at learning and adapting to change. The corporate world is still in the process of digesting the implications.

Henry Mintzberg – practical management thinker and contrarian
Mintzberg is a management professor at McGill University, Montreal and visiting scholar at INSEAD, Paris. Mintzberg is a wide-ranging management thinker who applies a very pragmatic approach to his studies. His most influential ideas include the surprising insight that senior managers have little time available for deep thought and that the bureaucratic planning process in many companies is not suitable for developing strategy. He believes that business schools are not giving managers enough training in practical aspects of management and has co-created a new course, the International Masters of Practical Management, to address the problem.

Michael Porter – corporate strategy with simple frameworks
Michael Porter is a professor at the Harvard Business School. His reputation stems from his work in understanding the nature of corporate strategy and distilling it into simple frameworks that managers can use to identify attractive markets, select strategies, decide which parts of the business to focus on and make the most of 'industry clusters'. Since the 1980s, his ideas have dominated corporate strategy.

Rosabeth Moss Kanter – corporate sociologist
Rosabeth Moss Kanter is a Harvard Business School professor, a former editor of the *Harvard Business Review* and was formerly a sociologist. Her most important contribution has been in examining the social pressures in organizations that aid or hinder competitiveness; in particular how large corporations can benefit from change, entrepreneurial principles and alliances. Her vision is of a highly flexible and 'empowered' workforce, freed from many of the divisional and role boundaries that make large companies resist change and that inhibit cooperation.

You couldn't ask to have a more talented team of people on your side.

2 Your Place in the Corporate World

Business creates wealth

Where would we be without business?

In the last 150 years, wealth has increased 20-fold or more in rich countries.

Want to get an idea of what it was like 150 years ago? Turn off all the lights. Unplug the stereo. Throw away the car keys. Turn off the fridge. Fill your house with smoke. And throw away most of your money. Better still, travel to one of the poorer countries in the world. India's wealth today is roughly where the US and UK were 150 years ago (see Fig. 2.1).

Who would go back to a life without modern conveniences – arduous hand washing, vitamin deficient dried foods, smoky, dangerous oil lamps, horses and carts, and country dancing for entertainment? Who would care to live without antibiotics, antiseptics, immunizations and other modern medical techniques? What few comforts were available then were painfully expensive. And few people had a political voice.

Largely we have business to thank for this unprecedented rise in our fortunes. The freeing up of business to allow private capital investment

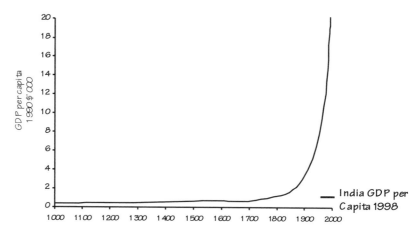

Fig. 2.1 GDP per person has grown rapidly in Western Europe over the last 200 years.

(stock exchanges and merchant banks), and the freedom to do business in any industry (general business incorporation), combined with a legal system supportive of enterprise (limited liability and legally enforceable contracts) have all allowed business to flourish (see Fig. 2.2). And, with business, has come technological innovation, efficient production, mechanization and the ability to manage large organizations.

It has been argued that scientific progress is the driving force behind the rapid growth. But without the prospect of business profits, there would have been far less incentive to innovate and turn ideas into useful products. And without these business successes, there would have been less money and less urgency for investigating the scientific mysteries.

In the rich countries, we're not rich because we have great science, a large population or great natural resources. We are rich because we can take those resources, people and ideas and create from them enormous amounts of value. To do that you need organization, you need to make sure resources are allocated to their most productive uses and you need

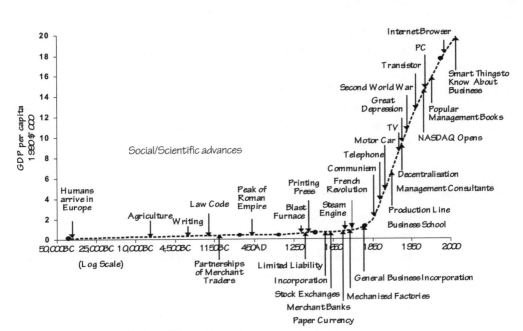

Fig 2.2 The take-off starts after a series of innovations in business form.

Smart quotes

'It is not from the benevolence of the butcher, the brewer, or the baker, that we expect our dinner, but from their regard to their own self-interest.

'[The individual] neither intends to promote the public interest, nor knows how much he is promoting it ... he intends only his own gain, and he is in this, as in many other cases, led by an invisible hand to promote an end which was no part of his intention ... By pursuing his own interest he frequently promotes that of the society more effectually than when he really intends to promote it.'

Adam Smith, *The Wealth of Nations*

an incentive to come up with better ways to provide value to people. In short you need a free and thriving business community.

And now that we have a productive business sector, we *expect* our wealth to grow by 2–3% every year. At that rate, in 100 years from now we'll all be ten times richer than today – imagine earning ten times what you do today!

Following a career in business

It's easy to think about society as being entirely separate from the world of business. But in reality our social lives are very much entwined with business. Not only do the products of business dominate the urban landscape, but business also provides most of our jobs.

Business is the most efficient system we know for turning our time, effort and knowledge into things we value. So it's not surprising that so many of us choose to work for businesses directly.

It's hard to generalize about careers in business. There are simply so many. After all, that's part of what makes business so efficient – the ability to combine the talents of many different trades. A typical business can employ more than 20 different kinds of specialists – factory technicians, logistics managers, IT managers, process engineers, market researchers, salesmen/account managers, customer service representatives, maintenance engineers, accountants, lawyers, HR managers, purchasing specialists etc. And within many of these, there are further distinctions of recognized specialities.

Even the career paths people follow are astonishingly different. The archetypal career path from factory floor to supervisor to manager is by no means the most typical or desirable today (Table 2.1).

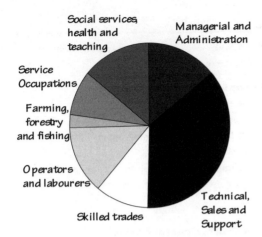

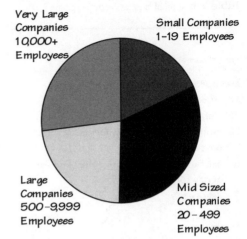

711 Listed Occupations, covering 135.2 million people
Source: US Bureau of Labour Statistics, 2000

Total Company Employees 110.7 million people
Source: US Census Bureau, 2000

Fig. 2.3 US employment by occupation.

Fig. 2.4 US employment by company size.

What kind of organization do you want to work for?

Just as important as the decision of which area of business to specialize in, is what kind of company you choose to work for.

Organization size is one factor. Small companies offer greater responsibility and a stronger sense of community and purpose. But small companies often have fewer opportunities for career development and fewer people to learn from. Large companies tend to offer more clearly defined career paths and more complex management systems.

What do you want from the company you work for?

Growth matters too. A fast-growing start-up offers excitement and opportunity. Slower-growth companies offer stability and greater sophistication in their marketing, production and management.

Culture matters too. Virgin is famous for its fun, young culture, while Microsoft is geek heaven. Shell offers a structured and professional approach to management development. The Body Shop unites its

Table 2.1 Typical business career paths

Typical career path	People who have achieved great success with a similar career path
Entrepreneur	**Richard Branson, Virgin Group**
18 Work for small clothing wholesaler	16 Starts business selling records
25 Start up own clothing import business	18 Starts Virgin records
30 Expand import business to include other luxury products	26 Millionaire. Starts diversifying into other businesses
50 Sell businesses. Invest in turnarounds of luxury goods companies	40 Billionaire. Virgin involved in wide diversity of businesses including drinks, airlines and finance
58 Retire early	
Engineer	**Jack Welch, General Electric**
24 Join a large industrial company as an engineer	24 Joins GE Plastics as a chemical engineer
33 Start up engineering consulting business	Promoted quickly to Business Unit manager
40 Join small industrial company as CEO	36 Youngest VP in GE history
50 Join a large manufacturer as COO	45 Chairman and CEO
55 Become a consultant to manufacturing companies	65 Retired
Sales and marketing	**Carly Fiorina, Hewlett-Packard**
21 Accounts manager for a large company	25 Joined AT&T as account manager
26 Regional sales manager, business unit	Promoted to various leadership positions in sales and marketing
29 One year break to work as market development manager in a start-up	42 President Lucent Technologies
30 Sales and marketing manager, business unit Promotions to larger business units	45 Chairman and CEO, HP
40 Business unit manager	
50 VP Marketing	
Finance	**Richard Wagoner, General Motors**
21 Join large accounting firm	25 Joined GM as Treasury Assistant
26 Specialize in corporate finance	30 Treasurer GM Brazil
30 Study for an MBA	36 VP and Finance Manager GM Canada
32 Join Finance Department of large corporate	Various Finance/Planning promotions
40 Become Head of Finance for a large division	40 CFO of GM
50 Become CFO of a medium-sized company	42 President GM North America
	48 President and CEO of GM

employees behind its ethical mission. Business offers so many choices – find a job that suits you.

How careers are changing

Careers in business are in a period of great change as we move from the late industrial bureaucracies of the post-war period to new forms of organization in which the role of the individual is more prominent (see box below).

Jobs increasingly involve problem solving rather than simple execution of repetitive duties. In part this reflects the greater specialization and complexity businesses need to compete today. And in part it's because routine processes are increasingly automated, freeing more employees to focus on creating value, rather than operating as a cog in the machine.

More jobs are technically skilled, involving a progression of competence, experience and knowledge. This progression can take place within a

Smart answers to tough questions

Q. How have careers in business changed over time?

A.
- *c.1800. Pre-industrial.* Tradespeople/hand-crafters working in guilds.
- *1800–1950. Early industrial.* Unskilled manual labourers concentrated in urban factories.
- *1930–present. Late industrial.* Complex organizational structures. Focus on scale and efficiency. Mix of skilled and unskilled labour supported by a large managerial/clerical staff.
- *1980–? Post industrial.* Greater specialization and need for training. Lean management. Project-based work and flexible roles.

> ### Smart people to have on your side: Peter Drucker and Rosabeth Moss Kanter
>
> *Empowerment*
> Empowerment is an important new management idea. Its leading promoters are Peter Drucker and Rosabeth Moss Kanter. Increasingly, senior managers are recognising that businesses are simply too complex for them to micro-manage alone. By empowering their workforce to take the initiative in solving business problems the management load is reduced and far more people can contribute to making the company operate more efficiently. For workers, it means more responsibility and less certainty, but also fewer restrictions, greater opportunities and more rewarding work.

single company or within a specialist department. But just as frequently, people gain their experience working for several different companies during their career.

Today, working for the same company for the entire duration of a person's career is something of a rarity. Freer labour laws have made it far easier to move from company to company. The emergence of temporary agencies for skilled workers has made it even easier to work with many different companies. Today many skilled workers can choose the jobs or projects they work on according to their interests and career needs. (See Chapter 17, 'The Future of Business' for more on these trends.)

> ### Smart things to say
>
> You can have it all – an interesting, rewarding career with the freedom to work towards your own goals.

No doubt, careers will continue to evolve. But for today's business workers, things are just getting more interesting.

PART I

Efficient Customer Value Creation

3 How do Companies Create Value?

It's all about efficient customer value creation

If there is only one thing you take away from this book, it should be the concept of *efficient customer value creation*. This principle is at the heart of business. It is so fundamental that we'd better make sure we understand it completely before moving on to all those fancy business theories we've heard so much about. Every one of them is just another method for achieving efficient customer value creation.

WARNING: THIS IS THE MOST IMPORTANT CHAPTER!

Molly is an entrepreneur about to start a new business. Obviously, top of her mind is making money for *herself*. She dreams of wealth and the magnificent lifestyle it will provide for her.

But who will the money come from and why will they give it to her?

Wealth will come from parting the vast sea of consumers from some of their hard-earned cash.

Smart quotes

'It is one of the most beautiful compensations of this life that no man can sincerely try to help another without helping himself.'

Ralph Waldo Emerson

Skipping past the option of theft, she'd better find something good to offer in exchange for those enticing green notes.

'Marketing thinking starts with the fact of human needs and wants.'

Philip Kotler

Molly must identify a customer need, and provide a valuable product or service. In this case, Molly is hoping to sell squeegee-mops that wash floors more quickly. The time saving being a valuable benefit that customers will hopefully be prepared to pay for.

By the same token, she will only make money if she is *efficient* at meeting this need. Unless the cost of making the squeegee-mops is less than the price she can charge, she'll be bankrupt before the year is out.

The more value she can create, the more she can charge. The more efficiently she can produce her mops, the lower her costs. So the key to making money is *efficient customer value creation*.

Creating customer value is about servicing needs not just providing products

Apparently, there is more than one way to skin a cat. And equally there is more than one way to create customer value.

It's tempting to think of business in terms of selling physical products. But this unnecessarily narrows the options for creating customer value.

To illustrate, let's follow Maria as she walks into a hardware shop in search of a hammer. The storeowner, looking for a quick sale, could take the narrow approach and try to sell her the cheapest, or best, or best-value-for-money hammer on the market. A more holistic approach would start by finding out what need Maria is seeking to meet.

Smart things to say

We can only make sustainable profits if we're really creating value for our customers and we're doing it more efficiently than anyone else can.

Smart answers to tough questions

Q: How can you get rich quicker?

A: Leverage – a recipe for riches
Once you've found one way to make money, exploit it to the maximum. Replicate your profit-making scheme over and over. If you can sell a mop to one person, how can you sell it to millions? If you can provide a useful service to one person, how can you provide it to everyone? If you have a great brand, how can you use it to sell more products? If you have a great technology, how can you use it to make more products more efficiently?

Increased size can often also make the business more profitable. Costs usually go down when you produce in greater quantities. An operation twice as large often doesn't need twice as much management, marketing or capital equipment. You can also get more bargaining power with suppliers and major customers.

But not all businesses *can* easily be scaled up. For example, how do you replicate your great people?

Sometimes even the most unlikely businesses can be replicated. Who would have thought it was possible to leverage a coffee shop? But by standardizing a great product, Starbucks Coffee has managed just that.

What customer need are you meeting and what is it worth to them?

Maria has recently been given a Japanese print for a present and would like to hang it on the wall. Her first instinct is to buy a hammer and a nail. But in fact, her need may be far better served by other means. Picture hooks may be more secure. Stick-on picture hangers may be cheaper and kinder to the masonry. And why buy a whole hammer when she only needs it for a single job? Why not hire a handyman to do it all for her? As an added bonus, she needn't put her thumbs at risk.

By focusing on how to service the need rather than just selling a product, the opportunities for value creation are far greater.

Smart quotes

'Manufacturers often make the mistake of paying more attention to their physical products than to the services produced by these products ... A physical object is just a means of packaging a service.'

Philip Kotler, Marketing Professor

A customer is not just a need

One can also be more subtle in examining customer needs. Again, a more holistic approach is valuable.

Chuffed with her success in the hardware store, Maria stops off next at clothes retailer Esprit to reward herself with a new sweater. Students who have mastered the ideas up to now will quickly analyse the problem according to needs:

- *Need*: Stay warm in cold weather

- *Solution*: Warm sweater

You might expect therefore that a cheap synthetic fleece would be the ideal solution. But this would completely misunderstand Maria's needs.

For most people, choosing clothes is not just about practicality. There is a great deal of social importance attached to appearance, so the dedicated follower of fashion will carefully select a sweater that sends all the right signals.

Additionally, clothes provide value through their sensual qualities. What could be better than the feel of a soft cashmere sweater?

And then, there is the act of shopping itself. The choosing. The social interaction. Being centre of attention. The decision. The unwrapping. And the excitement of the NEW thing.

Understanding all these additional needs gives the aspiring seller access to far more customer value than meeting the simple, superficial need.

Some stores know that the buying experience itself provides much of the value. Goods at Harrods department store in London command a higher price largely because of Harrods' exclusive image, rather than the quality of the goods themselves.

Smart quotes

'People no longer buy shoes to keep their feet warm and dry. They buy them because of the way the shoes make them feel – masculine, feminine, rugged, different, sophisticated, young, glamorous, "in". Buying shoes has become an emotional experience. Our business is now selling excitement rather than shoes.'

Francis C. Rooney, CEO HH Brown Shoe Co.

How to go about creating customer value

The next three chapters of the book look in more detail at the processes involved in creating customer value.

First, we look at the strategies available to companies for creating more customer value. We will see how customer value creation can be used to fend off that scourge of the entrepreneur: competition (Chapter 4, 'How to Meet Customers' Needs').

Then we start to look at the relationship between customers and companies in a little more detail. Most critical is whether customers trust the company to sell products that provide the value they advertised. Companies should recognize that trust has a financial value (Chapter 5, 'Earning the Customers' Trust').

Finally, we ask whether advertising can be effective in building a competitive advantage. Ideally, companies would like to influence customers' decision-making so that they buy *their* products (all else being equal). In practice, companies have very limited scope to gain a long-term advantage through influence. And what influence they can assert must be used very carefully for fear of undermining trust (Chapter 6, 'Persuading Customers to Buy Your Products').

Smart quotes

'The foundations of business have to be customer value and customer decisions on the distribution of their disposable income. It is with those that management policy and management strategy increasingly have to start.'

Peter Drucker

How to go about improving efficiency

Before we get to that, let's have a quick look at the other side of the equation – how to improve *efficiency*.

> 'There can be no economy where there is no efficiency.'
>
> Benjamin Disraeli

Efficiency matters a lot to companies. Clearly, the cost of manufacture needs to be lower than the customer value the product creates. Otherwise customers won't want to buy it for a profitable price and we can't make any money. But the price we can offer customers also needs to be lower than any of the alternatives available to them. It needs to be cheaper than customers servicing their own needs. It needs to be cheaper than alternative ways to meet their needs (so called 'substitute products'). And most importantly, it needs to be cheaper than the competition.

Molly, our intrepid entrepreneur, had better figure out how to produce those squeegee-mops at a competitive price.

> How efficient must we be to provide value to the customer and beat the competition?

There are two basic approaches to efficiency:

- technology investment; and

- specialization.

Efficiency gains from investing in technology

New technologies are an important source of efficient customer value creation. Many technologies meet old needs at a vastly reduced cost to the customer and also provide more customer value. Want to send a document to someone? You could send it by courier. But the postal system is cheaper. Fax machines are faster. E-mail is easier and cheaper still and provides an accurate electronic copy of the document.

New technologies are therefore useful because they allow us to get more from less.

But technology usually comes with a burden. Most (but not all) new technologies work on a common formula – invest a heap of money in machines, tools and training now, and reap the benefits later.

You could run a clothing factory in which people hand-sew all the garments, but it's much more efficient to buy sewing machines to do it. Sure, it costs more at first, but the saving in employee time more than compensates for the up-front cost.

Technology investment is the way most of our development occurs. Today an hour of a worker's time can produce ten times more than 150 years ago. The vast majority of that gain is possible due to cumulative investments in technology. Roads, cars, factories, computers, training etc. represent an enormous investment in technologies that let us do more for less, together providing us with enormous efficiency gains. But it doesn't come cheaply – if you wanted to set it all up again from scratch it would cost something like US$75,000 per person – or about 2.5 years worth of income for a rich country, or about 200 years of income for a very poor country.

The fact that we need to invest heavily in order to make use of a new technology has a huge impact on the economics of the business – the cost of serving even one customer is very large. But fortunately, the

Smart quotes

'Economic growth occurs whenever people take resources and rearrange them in new ways that are more valuable.'

Paul Romer, Growth Economist

incremental cost of the second, tenth, hundredth is very low. So now it pays to do things on a grand scale – big is efficient when it comes to technology investment.

Car factories are a good example of large-scale manufacturing. The investment in machinery, knowledge, design and infrastructure required to build a car is so high that it only pays if you are going to make a lot of them at the same time. So much so that only a few car manufacturing plants are likely to be needed to service all of North America's or Europe's demand for family cars.

Technology investment is a key source of efficiency and competitive advantage, but the economics of large-scale investment can lead to some difficult dilemmas for companies. (Chapter 7, 'Efficiency Gains from Technology Investment')

Efficiency gains from specialization

The other strategy for efficiency – specialization – is probably more familiar. A professional tradesman can sell his services because he is far more efficient than his customers can be. Certainly, there is some investment in tools involved, but most of the efficiency advantage comes because the tradesman has so much more experience, is better practised and often more skilled than his customer. I, for one, am perfectly willing to accept that a skilled carpenter is going to do a far better job of putting up shelves and in far less time than my talentless hands could ever manage.

Similarly, employees within companies specialize in skills they can be better at than anyone else in the organization.

Companies can benefit from specializing too. By concentrating in a few technologies, they can stay at the leading edge of industry practice.

Smart quotes

'The greatest improvement in the productive powers of labour ... seems to have been the effects of the division of labour. The great increase in the quantity of work ... is owing to the increase in dexterity in every particular workman; and to the saving of the time which is commonly lost in passing from one species of work to another.'

Adam Smith, *The Wealth of Nations*

Furthermore, being the best in a single specialized area helps to better communicate to potential customers what the company can do.

'Stick to your knitting.'

Tom Peters and Robert Waterman, *In Search of Excellence*

But while specialization has its advantages at a company-wide level, it's hard for a company to develop a core set of skills. It is a very different thing for an organization to 'learn' skills than for individuals. Companies must find ways to share knowledge and to use their skilled people effectively. Companies must find ways to take knowledge out of people's heads and make it available to everyone or the company will be forever limited by the productivity of a few people. This is what knowledge management is all about.

Chapter 8, 'Learning How to be More Efficient' looks at the ways companies can 'learn' from experience and use their knowledge efficiently.

How every step in the 'value chain' contributes to efficient customer value creation

For Molly, the technology of mop production is all a bit daunting and initially she hopes to sub-contract production to an experienced low-cost manufacturer. But this does not completely side step the issue of efficiency. Her subcontractor will face investment costs that will be

Smart people to have on your side: Michael Porter

The value chain as a strategic tool
Each step in getting from raw materials to meeting the customer need involves 'adding value' and, in theory, each step constitutes a business. Identifying which steps add the most value helps to identify which are the most strategically important. An understanding of the value chain ensures that companies are genuinely adding value at every step in their process and that they focus attention on those steps that add the most value.

passed on to Molly. And the sub-contractor's efficiency will be reflected in their prices, and therefore Molly's costs.

In producing almost any product or service, there are many steps from raw material to finished product. Each step costs money, but also contributes to the value of the product. These steps are known as the 'value chain'. At each step, materials are bought in, transformed and sold on to the next step in the chain.

Usually, the value chain for a product is spread over several companies, each specializing in their step of the value chain. Each company adds value and captures a portion of the total sales price of the goods.

Molly's value chain extends back far beyond her subcontractor. Her subcontractor will have to purchase aluminium tubes for the mop-handles, cloth for mop-heads and plastic to mould into the mop-heads. The cloth comes from a chemicals company that must buy oil to manufacture synthetic fibres before being woven into cloth. Along the way, machines are used, which are built by tool-making specialists from iron. The iron must be mined, processed and shaped by mining, refining and casting companies.

In our value chain, are we good at the activities that add most value?

Molly's simple idea requires the cooperation of a large interconnecting web of businesses. Without it, Molly's costs would be far, far higher.

The simplest steps in any value chain are the traders and shippers who live by the simple code of 'buy low – sell high'. Their 'value added' is to get products from where they are most efficiently produced to where they are needed.

So what is Molly's role in the value chain and what value is she adding?

Molly is buying the mops from her subcontractor and selling them on to her customers – so she is a trader of sorts. But she has also come up with a new kind of squeegee mop and adds value by contributing her idea to the value chain.

The subcontractor's contribution is crafting and assembling the mops.

Every step in the value chain serves its 'customer'

Every step in the value chain can be seen as a business whose aim is efficient creation of value for its 'customer'. For Molly's subcontractor, the customer is Molly herself. They can affect Molly's value a great deal. Of course, cheaper production allows lower costs, providing Molly with more profits. But they can also provide other benefits. For example, by responding more quickly to fluctuations in demand and delivering products in a more convenient way, they can reduce Molly's transport and stock-holding costs. They can also ensure that their production quality is high so that Molly's customers will be more satisfied and pay higher prices.

This need for every step in the value chain to create value for its customer next in the chain means that many of the principles we will apply to consumer goods apply equally to industrial products. In business there is no real distinction between a final consumer and an industrial customer so long as you accept that each has different needs and requires a different definition of customer value.

Achieving efficiency gains on a grand scale

For Molly's small entrepreneurial venture, management skills are not all that important. Molly can manage most tasks of running her operation herself or hire people to do things directly for her.

But as companies become bigger, their management needs become far more complicated. And costly.

Efficient management is just as important as efficient production.

For even quite small companies, management is a critical part of efficient customer value creation.

By making the right decisions, managers can ensure the company operates in the most attractive markets, sells the right products to the right people; and suffers fewer failures. Good management of innovation, product development, production technology and learning allows a company to improve efficient customer value creation faster.

Chapters 9 to 16 are concerned with how to manage companies. Chapter 9, 'How to Manage' asks what managers aim to do. The remaining chapters explore different aspects of management in detail.

Summary of main points

Phew! We've covered practically the whole of business theory in the last 15 pages. For now the main thing to remember is *efficient customer value creation:*

- create as much value for the customer as possible;

- make your processes as efficient as possible through technology investment and learning; and

- ensure every part of the value chain creates value efficiently.

4 How to Meet Customers' Needs

Seeing business from the customers' perspective

We're ready to launch into our money-for-services trade with customers. If we're going to get the most from it, we'd better understand the decision as far as possible from our customers' perspective. Remember, the more value we can create for our customers, the more cash they will be prepared to give up in return. And that's not going to happen until we know what it is they value.

We also saw that, for the customer, the buying experience is a complex and multi-faceted experience. The value of a product or service depends not just on the need being met, but also on other factors, such as aesthetics and social context. Furthermore, some of the value of a purchase is actually provided by the buying experience itself.

Smart quotes

'Marketing is so basic that it cannot be considered a separate function. It is the whole business seen from the point of view of its final result, that is, from the customer's point of view ... Business success is not determined by the producer, but by the customer.'

Peter Drucker

Smart people to have on your side: Philip Kotler

The customer-focused company
Kotler is professor of International Marketing at the Kellogg Graduate School of Management in Chicago. His book, *Marketing Management*, is *the* standard marketing textbook. Under Kotler's influence, marketing has shifted from a peripheral activity to the heart of a customer-focused company.

'The basic change in marketing thinking is the paradigm shift from *pursuing a sale* to *creating a customer*.'

'The customer is not a moron, she's your wife.'

David Ogilvy, Advertising Executive

So, if we want to provide the greatest possible value, we're going to have to understand our customers extremely well. We need to see the buying experience through their eyes. We're probably even going to have to spend a fair bit of time with them.

If Molly, our intrepid entrepreneur, is going to be selling those squeegee mops to housewives and professional cleaners, she's probably going to have to do some mopping herself.

'Our people are my first line of customers.'

Anita Roddick, Founder of The Body Shop

Too many companies fail to see the critical importance of seeing through their customers' eyes. Imagine a company of over-educated old men, trying to sell trendy nightclub gear to young, hip, teenage girls. It's not that rare! Now, can you imagine the marketing meetings? They might as well be talking about Martians![1]

Companies that take the customer-eye view seriously include the Body Shop and Virgin. Both strive hard to employ people who are similar to their customers. Both seem to have the knack of knowing what their customers will value.

Smart answers to tough questions

Q: How can you identify customer needs?

A: Focus groups

The idea of a focus group is absurdly simple. Gather some potential customers around a table to tell you what they want. It's such a simple idea, surely it hardly warrants a mention here!

But it's not quite so easy. Customers are notoriously bad at telling companies what they think. Often the context has a big impact on what they say – whether a new type of training shoe is 'cool' will depend to a large extent on whether the 'coolest' people wear it. Focus groups tend to be conservative and often fail to pick emerging trends. And focus groups have real problems in imagining how new ideas will work in practice.

Two focus group failures are worth a mention to demonstrate the problems. New Coke was the result of focus groups that suggested that people preferred a sweeter product, but they failed to consider what would happen if Coca-Cola messed with a cultural icon. Sony's Walkman was initially rejected by focus groups – fortunately Sony had confidence in their product.

Focus groups work best when they try to identify fundamental needs and attitudes. They fail most often when customers are asked to come up with new products. Design is best done by the company, not the customer.

It takes a lot of effort and a great deal of subtlety to get really useful results from focus groups. When they are used well, they can reveal great insights into customer thinking. Used badly, they are worse than useless.

Find out what the customer needs

Knowing about the customer helps. *Being* the customer is even better. But most companies find that understanding their customers' needs takes more than intuition; they really do have to do the research. With

Smart quotes

'[As Consumers] we may not always be able to describe the perfect fulfilment of our needs or the perfect solution to our problems, but we certainly know it when we see it.'

Rosabeth Moss Kanter

so much at stake, they can save a lot of money by knowing what will work before starting product development. Two useful techniques for analysing customers' needs are 'focus groups' and 'conjoint analysis'.

However, some companies aren't doing as much research any more. They face such rapid change and uncertainty that they cannot afford to spend a great deal of time and money on customer research. Instead, they realize that the best way to find out what works is to just go and try it out in the market.

Smart answers to tough questions

Q: How can you measure customer needs?

A: Conjoint analysis

Conjoint analysis is far more sophisticated. It tries to *measure* customer value – it puts a dollar value on each of a product's features.

Customer value is not an easy thing to measure, but the conjoint approach is rather smart. It gives people a series of choices between two products – each representing a package of features. For example, the customer might be asked to choose between two cars: a Turbo convertible with sports-car performance and air conditioning for $15,000 against a non-air conditioned, fuel-efficient sedan for $8000. After about ten such choices, a computer can calculate the relative value the customer places on each of the various attributes.

All this assumes that people's preferences are linear and consistent, but in reality they rarely are. For example, in valuing the features of a car, speed is not always going to be worth the same to a customer. If a car costs under $6000 it's 'just another car' and price, reliability and economy will be important; speed will be worth relatively little. But at $80,000, the car is 'for keeps' and it is valued as much for its role as a status symbol and a form of recreation as for its practicality. Suddenly, speed becomes a much more important factor.

Still, conjoint is a useful tool because even if it fails to accurately model individual decisions, it provides some good rules of thumb for the customer-base as a whole, allowing companies to make useful trade-offs. For example, which features will the customer pay more for? When profits depend on getting these decisions right to within a couple of percentage points, conjoint analysis provides hard data to help make the right decisions.

Smart people to have on your side: Philip Kotler

Experimental product development
According to Kotler, product development in the 1980s was characterized by: 'Ready! Aim! Fire!' – Create the product, do the market research, then sell the product.

Greater sophistication in customer research in the 1990s led to: 'Aim! Ready! Fire!' – Do the research first and develop the products as a result.

In the 21st century, he hypothesizes, it will be: 'Fire! Fire! Fire!' – No time for research, just go and try it!

How to compete for customers

It's about time we got around to considering one big complication. We've avoided it so far, but sooner or later we're going to have to deal with ... COMPETITION.

Sadly, we're not generally going to have the customer to ourselves. For most customer needs, there will be many companies hoping to convert a value-creating opportunity into cash. So we'd better start figuring out how we are going to deal with these interlopers.

Competition greatly reduces profits for businesses

For one thing, competition is going to seriously reduce the price we can charge for our services.

It's no longer just the company and the customer negotiating over how to share out all that value we've just created for them. If our product created $100 of value for the customer, then if it were just between them and us, we might persuade the customer to part with $70, even if it only cost $40 for us to produce. That's a tidy profit of $30 for us, and $30 of value for the customer. Everyone's a winner!

How can we avoid direct competition?

With competition, things get a bit tougher for us. A competitor is going to want their share of the action. If we are charging $70, they could win over our entire customer base at a price of $60 – still netting them a tidy $20 per customer. We'd have to cut prices even lower to get anything at all. Finally we'll get to a point where we split the market, but neither competitor makes any money at all – each selling a product for a price of $40, that costs $40 to make. The customer though is laughing, taking home a product providing $100 of value for just $40 – customers just love competition.

In perfectly competitive markets, prices will always fall to the point at which no one makes money. If you want to make a profit, you need to be able to either charge a higher price or produce more efficiently than your competitors.

The solution for companies, it seems, is to avoid fair, equal competition at all costs. This is the theme for the rest of this chapter.

How to avoid competition

Business is a competition for customers. You win when a customer chooses your services over those of your competitors. You make money when you can win customers while still selling at a price higher than your costs.

The customer is the only judge that matters.

To get the customer to choose your services over those of your competitors you need to convince them that your product offers them more value for money.

Smart people to have on your side: Michael Porter

Generic strategies for competitive success
Michael Porter gives three generic approaches to competitive success:

- niche focus;
- differentiation; and
- cost leadership.

According to Porter, companies should concentrate on just one of these strategies. Companies attempting to balance more than one of these strategies are likely to fail because products will be poorly positioned in customers' minds and the mixed strategy will create internal conflicts. Porter refers to this dysfunction as being 'stuck in the middle'.

Two of Michael Porter's three generic strategies (see box above) concern how to use customer value to compete – niche focus and differentiation:

- *Niche focus* – A niche focus strategy aims to provide more value to a particular group of customers (a market 'segment'). This strategy recognizes that different people have different needs. So a product that caters to the needs of one market segment should be able to produce more value to these customers than one aimed at the market as a whole.

- *Differentiation* – The aim is to try to encourage customers to *perceive* your product as being different. By focusing on one feature, you aim to capture all the customers for whom that feature is most important.

Porter's third strategy, cost leadership, is to offer the same product for a lower price. For such a strategy to work effectively in a competitive environment, it is necessary to be able to produce at a lower cost. We will look at how companies can use production efficiency to compete in Chapter 7, 'Efficiency Gains from Technology Investment' and Chapter 8, 'Learning How to be More Efficient'. In this chapter, we focus only on customer value based approaches to competition.

Niche focus and differentiation look similar – both target customers whose needs are different from the rest of the market. But they are two different ways of achieving this.

A *niche focus* strategy selects customers by *who they are*. The company sets out to meet the particular needs of a customer segment. By focusing on just this group of customers, the company can understand their needs better, and often reduce marketing costs by targeting promotion to a narrower market.

For example, French hotel group, Formule 1 focuses on the needs of one segment: low-budget domestic business travellers. It locates its hotels near major transport routes, and has designed its hotels around providing only those services that these customers value most. Formule 1 used conjoint analysis extensively in the design of its hotel format to ensure they met as many of their target customers' needs as possible at the lowest possible price.

By contrast, a *differentiation* strategy selects customers by *what they value*. There is no reason why the customers should have anything in common apart from the importance they place on a certain product characteristic.

For example, in the copier market Canon differentiates itself as having the highest quality product, while Xerox has attempted to sell itself as the technology leader. A small graphic design company and a large pharmaceutical company may both opt for the perceived technological benefits of a Xerox product, despite the fact they are very different types of customer with very different needs, united only by the importance they place on technology.

In addition to Porter's strategies, we can add another strategy based on customer value:

● *Innovation leadership* – the company invents new and better ways to provide more customer value. Ideas are generally easy to copy, so leadership can only be maintained by consistently innovating.

Avoid competition: niche focus/segmentation

How do we decide whether a niche focus strategy might make sense for our company?

Smart quotes

'A company that decides to operate in a broad market recognizes that it normally cannot serve all customers in that market … Companies are increasingly embracing target marketing.'

Philip Kotler

Smart people to have on your side: Philip Kotler

Five characteristics of effective segments
According to Kotler, to be effective a strategy based on niche focus will only work for those segments that have the following five characteristics:

- *substantial* – large enough to be profitable to serve;
- *accessible* – can be effectively served and reached;
- *differentiable* – can be distinguished by their behaviour;
- *actionable* – there is a way to take advantage of their different needs; and
- *measurable* – can monitor progress to enable effective planning.

According to Kotler (see box above), there are five characteristics that define an effective market segment. These can be explained more simply as:

How can we use differences in customer needs to our advantage?

- there must be a big difference between different customers' needs;

- the additional cost of serving a narrower market, or several markets, must be small enough for it to be worthwhile; and

- there must be an effective way to market specifically to our target segment.

If a potential segment meets these three criteria, it is usually worthwhile to treat it as a separate niche market.

The impact of market maturity on segmentation

These three factors often depend on how mature an industry is. As an industry matures, it usually becomes much easier to segment the market.

When a new breakthrough technology occurs, it can often provide a better value-for-money prospect for the whole market. In comparison, differences in customer needs are relatively small and the cost of serving several customer segments is relatively high.

As the market matures, the potential for segmentation increases. The market as a whole is larger, meaning that it is easier to produce efficiently for several segments. As competition increases the value for customers, the differences in customers' needs become more apparent.

A good example of this behaviour is the car industry. Ford's Model T was first produced in 1908. Its production line manufacturing process created a large cost advantage that allowed it to win most of the car market, and lower costs meant substantial growth. By the 1930s the market was large enough and needs different enough that GM could target different products at different customer segments and win most of the market from Ford. GM could produce on a large enough scale to reap most of the production efficiencies Ford enjoyed, but could design models to meet the needs of specific customer groups – in GM's words, 'a car for every wallet'.

Today the proliferation of car models is far greater. A larger car market and more flexible manufacture has enabled car makers to target even smaller customer segments.

Car makers are looking at going a step further still. Their aim is 'mass customization'. In principle it will be possible to tailor an individual car to an individual customer's needs. Already, test factories are being built in which the final configuration of a car can be determined on the production line in response to a customer order and be delivered to the customer in a couple of days.

Smart answers to tough questions

Q: How has market maturity affected segmentation in the car industry?

A:
- Stage 1 – Revolutionary cost breakthrough. In 1908, the Ford Model T production line allowed a big price advantage, but 'any colour so long as it's black'.
- Stage 2 – Cost benefits mostly achievable at a smaller scale. In the1930s GM created five major divisions, providing 'a car for every wallet'.
- Stage 3 – Maturity. Today there is a far wider array of segments – SUVs aimed at active lifestylers, small cars aimed at city convenience, space wagons aimed at families etc.
- Stage 4? – Mass customization. The near future – cars built to order at mass-production prices.

Will mass customization be the way of the future for mature industries?

Mass customization will only work if mass-production costs are achieved while maintaining a high level of customization.

One approach to keeping costs low is to mass-manufacture standard parts that can be assembled in a variety of different ways. Dell does this in building PCs to order. Another approach is to mass-manufacture standard models, which can be altered superficially to meet customers' needs. Nokia does this with its cellular phones, using clip-on covers and downloadable ring-tones.

A second challenge is helping customers choose what they want. Too much choice can be daunting and time-consuming for customers. Furthermore, what they want may turn out to be impractical to produce. So companies must produce easy-to-use selection and design tools that take production limitations into account. An example of this is in custom-designed silicon chips where chip fabricators have moved from expensive joint-design to creating computer-based tools for customers to use themselves. The reduction in costs for customers is so big that it has created a much larger market for custom-designed chips.

The benefits of a company focusing on one segment

There is nothing stopping a company from separately appealing to several different customer segments at one time with different products (usually under different brands, or sub-brands). But unless there are compelling reasons to target several segments at a time (e.g. production efficiencies), companies often find that they do best when they focus on a single customer segment.

Single segment focus means that the company can match its culture to its customers, employees understand the customers' needs and the company can focus its attention on a single brand. Target customers learn that the company focuses on their needs. Costs are often reduced by focusing on marketing channels and market research specific to the target group. And a focus on one customer group can help align priorities within the company.

Artificial segmentation

Some companies have managed the trick of creating segmentation where customers' needs are not necessarily very different. The reason for doing so is that customers receive additional value just from knowing that products are specifically designed for them; and so that customers can be separated on the basis of their willingness to pay.

One example is the 'feminine razor' for use by women to shave their legs. Functionally, of course, it is indistinguishable from its male facial counterpart. But by separating the male and female markets, a higher price can be charged and women perceive that their particular needs are being met.

Identifying and targeting a segment

In our assessment of what makes an effective segment, we pointed out that it is also necessary to be able to market specifically to a target segment.

This turns out to be quite hard. How do they know you can meet their particular needs better? How can you be sure they are the ones who respond to your marketing messages? And how do you avoid wasting money advertising to and serving customers outside your target group?

An inability to separate targeted customers from the rest of the market is generally fatal for a niche focus strategy. Therefore, an important part of implementation is to find ways to signal to your target customers that this product is for them.

There are a few general approaches you can use:

- *Differentiation* – using product features/attributes that are particularly highly valued by your target segment.

- *Brand image* – using a brand image that appeals particularly to the target segment.

- *Channels* – use of advertising/sales/distribution channels that the target-customers use frequently, or which appeal particularly to them.

- *Behaviour* – use behavioural differences to separate customers.

Airlines are particularly sophisticated at accessing different segments separately. Airlines are in the business of artificial segmentation – their customers want essentially the same product (air transport from one place to another), but airlines know that it pays to segment customers to exploit differences in their willingness to pay.

What makes airlines special, though, is how sophisticated they are at separating out each of their segments – they use every trick in the book. They use service differentiation to separate price insensitive business passengers (the additional cost of better meals, wider seats etc. is far lower than the additional price they can charge). Behavioural differences can be exploited by raising prices for last-minute bookings, separating out passengers who have an urgent need to travel. Brand differences are used – there are separate brands for 'First Class' and 'Executive Class'. Advertising differences – very different advertising is used in business magazines. And channel differences – with different prices for different travel agencies and for Internet bookings. As a result, airlines often manage to charge 20 or more different fares for the same flight!

Avoid competition: differentiation/positioning

As we've seen, differentiation is about signalling to customers that your product is different from those of competitors. It is about *positioning* the product in the customer's mind. To do this you need a simple, unique message that expresses succinctly what your product can do for customers.

Customers tend to simplify their decision-making – instead of wasting time in detailed product assessments and comparison shopping, they would look for the product that appears to meet their most important needs. So it pays for companies to communicate in the same way – giving a clear indication of what is special about their product.

To give an example, many sports cars advertise their 0–60 acceleration and top speed. In themselves, these attributes are not likely to matter a great deal to a prospective buyer – whiplash is whiplash, and sports cars rarely ever get the chance to reach their top gear. And other factors are likely to be just as important to customers – comfort, cornering, braking etc. But the important thing about speed and acceleration is what they signal – uncompromising design priorities.

Thus differentiation is a way to make one attribute stand for everything the product will deliver.

Unique or superlative claims work best: they are more easily remembered. (Who ever remembers who came second?) When the battle for customers is principally conducted inside the mind of the customer, it is worthwhile carving out a unique space for your product.

Of course, you need to back up your claim. It's no good positioning yourself as being the 'best quality' if your products can't live up to the boast.

Smart people to have on your side: Al Ries and Jack Trout

Positioning
Ries and Trout are two advertising executives who popularized the idea of product 'positioning'. They argued that products have a unique position in the mind of consumers that helps the consumer know when that product might be useful to them. Companies must therefore look to create a unique position for their products in their customers' minds.

Hertz is well known as the biggest car rental company. Avis, number two in the market, is therefore likely to hold a low level of customer attention in comparison. But Avis's message is 'We try harder' – turning a potential negative of positioning (being #2) into a positive (therefore we provide better service).

'Positioning is not what you do to a product. Positioning is what you do to the mind of the prospect.'

Make your position the most important one

It is one thing to claim a unique position in the customers' minds. However, your position must also appeal to a large number of potential customers. Clearly it's necessary to try to stake a claim to the position that will appeal to the greatest number of customers.

But companies pursuing a differentiation strategy also have the opportunity to demonstrate that the position they hold is the one that matters most. This is an idea we will return to in Chapter 6, 'Persuading Customers to Buy Your Products'.

Avoid competition: innovation leadership

The final approach to avoiding competition is to improve your product so that it offers more value to customers. That means finding new ways to meet customer needs. It requires some serious creativity.

Creativity isn't an easy thing to build into an organization. Committees are famously incapable of creativity. Fortunately, there are techniques that help even corporate committees think creatively (see the box on p. 48).

But creativity is an inherently uncertain process. You can't *plan* to have a new idea. And you can't predict when great market breakthroughs will come along. But you can increase the chances of coming up with a good idea by putting as many brains on the job as possible. The more open the company is to ideas from unusual sources, the better.

Killer question: a quick test of your creative powers

How do you prevent tools and equipment from floating around in a spacecraft, while keeping them handy? (See endnote[2] for the answer.)

Smart people to have on your side: Edward de Bono

Lateral thinking
Edward de Bono wants to make people more creative. For De Bono, creativity is about freeing problem solving from mental constraints, and he has come up with a series of techniques that aim to do just that.

In one creativity technique, for example, a problem is reframed in an unfamiliar context to encourage new ways of looking at it.

In one approach to problem solving, De Bono separates the creative process into six separate modes of thinking, separating creativity from practical constraints and doubts for example, so that good ideas aren't abandoned for trivial reasons, and bad ideas get the chance to inspire better ones.

Companies that rely on innovation are increasingly looking to De Bono for inspiration.

Customers care a lot about how companies meet their needs – so solicit their ideas. Employees who live and breathe the product are likely to be an untapped source of ideas. Ideas from other industries can often be adapted. And look to your most demanding customers to tell you what they want.

With all those potential idea generators on hand, why do companies restrict themselves to the grey men in dark suits locked away in the distant centres of the organization?

Creating an organization that encourages participation and creativity is a tough challenge. Some management thinkers feel that 'empowerment' of employees and more decentralized decision-making will help to foster greater creativity too. (We'll look again at the benefits of empowerment in Chapter 10, 'How to Delegate' and Chapter 15, 'How to Manage Change'.)

Smart quotes

'Well-managed companies are not only close to their customers, they search out and focus on their most demanding customers.'

Andrew H. Van de Ven, Marketing Professor

And we had better not just make small incremental gains. Give customers a *big* reason to change. Revolutionize the industry! Don't just try to tip the balance of the customer decision, make it a complete no-brainer.

And you're going to have to *keep* coming up with new ideas if you're going to stay one step ahead of the competition.

Start a revolution!

It's often easy for competitors to copy a good idea. A new product might only have a shelf-life of a year before someone copies it or comes up with something better. So you're going to need a couple of big new ideas every year if you want to stay ahead.

If anything, the rate at which big ideas are needed is getting ever faster. Companies are learning that it pays to be able to cut the lead-time on development.

To be successful at a strategy of innovation leadership, companies need to become excellent at the processes of innovation, product

Smart quotes

'Doing what was done yesterday, or doing it 5% better is no longer a formula for success. Major changes are necessary to survive and compete effectively.'

John Kotter, Change Guru

development and launching new products; to become super-creative and fast-moving. (For more on the process of innovation see Chapter 7, 'Efficiency Gains from Technology Investment'.)

Summary of main points

- To meet customers' needs, you need to understand what's valuable to them and how they make decisions

- To make profit in a competitive industry, companies need to offer customers more value or be able to produce more cheaply. There are three strategies available for avoiding direct competition based on creating more customer value:

  - *Niche focus* – focus on serving a particular customer segment.
  - *Differentiation* – position the product in the customer's mind as being distinct from competitors' offerings.
  - *Innovation leadership* – use innovation to keep finding new ways to provide more value to customers.

Notes

1   Some companies hire 'cool hunters' or 'industrial anthropologists' to help them better understand their young customers. But the corporatization of a fashion risks making it instantly unfashionable, and many companies have found themselves chasing their tails.

2   NASA invented Velcro to solve precisely this problem!

5 Earning the Customers' Trust

The importance of customers' trust

So now we know how to identify our customers and meet their needs. But customers must be convinced that the product will actually deliver and their doubts must be quelled.

Will the product actually do what it should do? Will it last a reasonable amount of time before it breaks? If I have a problem, will the company be responsive in helping me? Can I be sure I won't have to pay more than other people?

And how should the customer decide *which* company to trust?

There are a few clues that will help a customer to decide:

- her previous purchases from the company;

- the company's apparent commitment to their product;

- the impression she gets from the company's image/reputation; and

- how well she trusts the company's representatives (e.g. sales staff).

Trust is a big issue in a customer's purchase decision. It isn't just a matter of being concerned about being conned – after all customers have legal resources and companies will usually do the right thing eventually when faced with an irate customer willing to kick up a fuss.

But why would anyone want to go through all that hassle? Most customers are willing to pay a premium to know they can trust a company. And if they don't trust that the product will deliver, then they'll need a big discount before they'll be tempted to take a risk.

So trust is worth money to companies – the more trusted they are, the more they can charge for their products and the more likely it is that customers will choose their products.

Of course, it's hard for companies to convince people that they're trustworthy. *Of course you say you're trustworthy. But can you prove it?*

The role of past experience and gossip in building trust

How past experiences affect trust

The best guide to how a company will behave is the customer's past experience with them. Companies that have been good to deal with in the past can usually be trusted again.

Companies will often bend over backwards to win the trust of their customers. For example, Nordstrom in the US cites a famous instance where a customer complained that a tyre the company sold them was faulty – Nordstrom's reaction was to refund the customer immediately. Great! But Nordstrom doesn't even sell those tyres! Similarly, Marks & Spencer, a UK retailer, allows customers to return any item for any reason, no questions asked.

These examples seem absurd. From the company's point of view it is clearly uneconomical to be so generous. But for the customer it provides a clear example of the trustworthiness of the company – that they will do what is right over what is profitable. And that is a strong source of trust.

This generosity is not nearly as altruistic as it appears – companies *know* that it's also profitable. Satisfied customers who return over and over again provide a great deal of profit over time. The company dare not jeopardize the huge amount of future value with a momentary breach of trust today. Long-term customer relationships are naturally trust building, because both sides have strong incentives to preserve the value of future interactions.

How gossip affects trust

Gossip! Gossip might seem frivolous, but it provides people with a useful way to keep tabs on trustworthiness. A delighted customer will tell their friends. So tapping into gossip is a great way for a company to build trust.

What do our customers say about us to their friends?

The converse is even truer. News of a bad experience spreads like wildfire. As a rule of thumb, marketing professionals work on the basis that a single bad experience has a negative effect on ten potential customers. And that was before the Internet allowed disgruntled customers to spread the word to millions!

Avoiding dissatisfaction is more important than delighting customers. Bad experiences make for much better gossip – there's just more drama in it. Certainly a good disaster story is better than: 'I bought a new toothbrush today – it was really pretty good – you can really trust those Oral-B toothbrushes.' It hardly makes for riveting conversation. And toothbrush evangelism might just be taken as a sign of insanity!

The importance of commitment in building trust

A company that backs its claims with its wallet is clearly demonstrating its confidence in its products. Money-back guarantees, lowest-price guarantees and unquestioned returns policies are commitments that engender trust. For the company, the news is even better – very few people ever actually take advantage of guarantees. After a customer has bought the product it's a pain to take it back – it's easier just to chalk it up to experience. But a company is doing even better if they never give the customer a reason to complain.

Another kind of commitment is advertising. Customers appreciate that only the biggest products could possibly justify a large advertising campaign. And if the company is so sure about the product's success, it must have something valuable. The commitment value of advertising may even be more important than the persuasive power of the advertising message.

No wonder Internet companies were so keen on advertising. What could be less tangible than an Internet company? Advertising is one of the few serious commitments these companies can make.

For bricks and mortar companies, commitment can also come in the form of major investments such as building large factories – often a strong signal of commitment in industrial markets.

How brands build trust

Brands are all about conveying trust. By branding a product, the company makes it easier for customers to relate previous experiences to new purchases. You liked Kellogg's Corn Flakes? Well, you know what to look for next time you go shopping. And you'll probably like Kellogg's Rice Crispies too. Branding shows confidence – companies won't risk their brand's reputation with shoddy products.

A great brand name, such as Coca-Cola, is worth a great deal to a company.

Brands also provide additional cues to trustworthiness. People use personality as an important guide to trustworthiness when evaluating other people. But when dealing with companies – what personality do you assign to a faceless monolithic profit-centred organization? Probably not a particularly trustworthy one!

So brands seek to provide the company with a more attractive personality. KFC's Colonel Sanders is a clear effort to give personality to a company. He embodies the stereotype of the Southern gentleman – warm, generous, down-to-earth, well presented and honest. Not a bad combination to reflect homely comfort food of consistent quality. (More recently, he's been reinvented with 'attitude', reflecting the changing priorities of a now overwhelmingly 'youth' customer-base.)

How do people see our brand? Is it consistent with our behaviour, our services and our customers?

Other brands are playful, some stylish. In each case, the brand becomes closely identified with a personality. Companies must also behave in a way that reflects the personality of the brand. Sales staff for a fun brand should be fun to deal with. Creative brands should reflect their playfulness in experimental advertising and product development – even if the new ideas don't work, they reinforce the brand image.

Brands can go further still. Nike has transcended the need to refer to the customer's world to gain credibility. Instead Nike's customers can refer to the *brand* to generate credibility for themselves. This is revolu-

Smart people to have on your side: Al Ries

22 immutable laws of branding
Al and Laura Ries give their rules for creating successful world-class brands in their book, *The 22 Immutable Laws of Branding*. Its main message is that a brand must be focused, consistent and different.

tionary indeed! Nike has created a unique personality from a mixture of stylishness and idealistic slogans. It hasn't been averse to associating with iconic sporting figures to add respectability. Although even here things are not as simple as they seem – the Nike brand and the athlete's brand (even athletes have brands nowadays) are mutually reinforcing. And Nike's commitment to advertising has made its brand a powerful and ubiquitous cultural reference in its own right.

Smart people to have on your side: Philip Kotler

Deep brands
A 'deep brand' is one that is strongly understood by customers at six levels of meaning: attributes, benefits, values, culture, personality and users.

Smart people to have on your side: Naomi Klein

Have brands gone too far?
The success of Klein's book, *No Logo*, an anti-brand rant, is a sign that perhaps branding has gone too far. *No Logo* makes a number of complaints against consumer products companies. The most potent are:

- that brands and brand advertising have become so pervasive they are corrupting and dumbing-down the arts and invading our social spaces without public consent; and
- brands give a very false impression of the (generally poor) ethics, values and behaviours of the companies behind them.

Nike's model is one that more companies want to replicate. But how many of these mega-brands can people take? They are already intertwining themselves so closely with social meaning that the very reality of sports, arts and culture are being questioned – a phenomenon that scares a lot of people. Already much of the cultural landscape of the world has become shockingly branded.

Smart answers to tough questions

Q: How much is a brand worth?

A: Brands have a measurable value. The Coca-Cola Company is worth more than PepsiCo on a can-for-can or even a profit-for-profit basis. Much of the difference can be attributed to the strength of the Coca-Cola brand. But why should a good brand be more valuable? Investors *should* only care about returns, so what value can a brand provide to them?

- Brands allow companies to charge their customers higher prices.
- Brands persist in customers' minds so companies can spend less on advertising without suffering an immediate decline in market share.
- Brands reduce risk – a bad product decision has less effect on a strong brand than a weak one.
- Brands can be extended to boost new products.
- A company that has learned to develop one strong brand often has the skills to develop others.

To illustrate the value of the Coca-Cola brand, we can look back to the 'New Coke' fiasco. For most companies a failed product revitalization would have been an expensive disaster. But for Coke, it might actually have improved Coca-Cola's performance. When 'Classic' Coke was reintroduced, it reminded people of their commitment to Coke – the icon.

Are customers loyal?

Loyalty is an even more desirable customer trait than trust. A loyal customer trusts you, but is unlikely to trust a competitor. For the company, loyal customers have some very attractive behaviours:

- loyal customers seek out the company's products, so advertising and promotion costs are reduced;

- loyal customers are more tolerant of experiments and occasional mistakes, so risks of innovation and new product development are reduced; and

- loyal customers will readily try new ideas, so new product launches are likely to be more successful.

But do loyal customers really exist?

The kinds of behaviour described above are very rare. Customers show a distinct readiness to switch suppliers when more value can be obtained elsewhere. The reasons are:

- customers' loyalty is rarely rewarded since companies have little awareness of an individual customer's behaviour; and

- companies have a strong incentive to exploit customers' loyalty through higher prices and poor service.

But loyalty represents an enticing opportunity. If a company can be trusted *not* to exploit loyalty and demonstrates an ability to notice and reward it, perhaps they can secure a benefit.

One approach is to create a long-lasting personal relationship with a salesperson. This works when there are relatively few customers (e.g.

Airbus sales representatives work hard to build relationships with individual airlines).

When there are many customers, technology can increasingly help track customer behaviour and solicit feedback (e.g. Amazon.com tracks its customers' purchases and uses the information to provide value-added services and offer incentives for loyalty).

How to lock-in customers

But what about all those 'loyalty schemes' companies foist on their customers? These schemes have very little to do with loyalty and everything to do with 'lock-in'.

Companies aim to make it uneconomical for their customers to switch to a competitor. For example, once you have been a customer with a bank for some time, you find that you have multiple accounts, direct debits set up and other special arrangements. Switching to another bank is so hard that most customers are practically captives. Banks can exploit this with high costs and poor service. The point at which customers finally switch is surprisingly high. Far from being loyal, bank customers in most countries resent their banks.

The trick to successful lock-in is to make the relationship so deep and multifaceted that a switching decision becomes too difficult to contemplate. A common trick is for the company to know so much about you that it would be painful to begin a new relationship elsewhere.

Frequent-flyer schemes are even less subtle. The idea is to reward frequent flyers with free flights. In effect, it reduces the cost of flying, so long as you stick with one airline. As a result, customers find themselves locked-in. (Interestingly, the customers that airlines really want to keep – the very frequent travellers – are the hardest to lock-in

Smart answers to tough questions

Q: How does Amazon.com lock-in its customers?

A: While most dot.com enterprises have foundered, Amazon.com has been successful. The main reason for this success has been that customers keep coming back – and Amazon has tried hard to find ways to lock-in customers.

Amazon's 1-Click™ ordering system ensures that once personal information is entered, ordering is quick. Customers attempting to switch to another site must invest a good deal of time re-entering their personal details and learning to navigate the new site. Additionally, Amazon's Recommendation Centre tracks previous purchases and suggests new books likely to interest buyers – the greater the proportion of books a customer buys on Amazon, the more valuable the service will be.

since they travel enough to accumulate top-tier benefits from several different airlines.)

Lock-in is akin to monopoly – something we will look at in some detail in a later chapter (Chapter 12, 'Creating a Lasting Competitive Advantage'). Once you lock-in a customer, you have the opportunity to avoid competition and can make far more money.

In common with monopoly, the avoidance of competition through lock-in schemes is a double-edged sword. Lack of competition can lead to inefficiency, slowness and customer resentment. Resentment that remains pent-up until the monopoly is broken (e.g. other airlines offer to redeem your points on their airlines, or banks offer to take over the administrative problems of transferring account information for you).

Nevertheless, lock-in is a source of great value for companies and a key strategy for success.

Summary of main points

OK, so what does it all mean in terms of efficient customer value creation?

- Trust creates value for customers, which can be translated into higher prices.

- Trust can be developed by good past experiences, demonstrated commitment and through a positive brand image.

- 'Loyalty' is something of a misnomer – it is usually means either:

  - reciprocation for value already received; or
  - 'lock-in' – where higher profits can be made from a customer's inability to switch to a competitor.

6 Persuading Customers to Buy Your Products

How to get the message across to customers

So far we have assumed that customers know what they want and that they choose the best available product or service. But if it were as simple as that, why would companies spend so much money on advertising?

You only get one chance to make a first impression.

Companies have very few ways to communicate with customers. Advertising is the easiest way to reach a large group of people cost effectively with a message. But what should that message be?

The first thing that companies need to communicate to customers is that there is a product out there that can meet their needs.

If we tried to summarize our key message in one sentence, what would it be?

Advertisers realize that people need to be reminded of their needs – people can need/want something for a long time, but won't act until their attention is called to it. Advertisers seek to call attention to your needs at exactly the right moment to make you go out and buy their product.

But advertising is a pretty blunt instrument – advertisers must continually bombard people with their advertising message in the hope that they can get their message across to the right people at the right time. Confronted with this barrage, people tend to ignore advertising.

Ideally, advertisers would like to know exactly when a customer will make a purchase decision and only then provide an appropriate message. Examples of such context-specific targeting are specialist magazines, which people often consult before making a purchase; and advertising near shops, so that as the customer goes to make a purchase, they can be reminded of the value-creating potential of a particular product.

The dangers of the 'hard sell'

As we will see, it *is* possible in the short term to use various influencing techniques to alter people's buying behaviour in useful ways. However, people do generally know what creates value for them. When they are influenced into doing something that is not in their interests, they resent it. Ultimately the company loses out because resentment destroys trust.

Can advertising actually make you buy a product you wouldn't otherwise want?

So, in general, the 'hard sell' is self-defeating – it gains one quick sale but loses a long-term relationship and generates bad word of mouth. (Some industries such as life insurance are notorious for hard-sell tactics, because word of mouth and relationships are relatively unimportant.)

This is an important but frustrating paradox of marketing. Customers have one decision-making criterion for making a purchase decision and another for judging the success of the product – influencing their future decisions. So do you win lots of customers by influencing their initial purchase decision or do you provide the best possible product and rely on customers to discover the true value of your product?

Companies looking to the long-term should generally focus on providing customer value. But it may take a while to become successful – time that companies don't always have. It was no use to Van Gogh that his paintings were finally appreciated after he was dead! If only one of his *Sunflowers* paintings could have sold for $40 million in his own lifetime.

The company looking to build trust in the long term must therefore try to do the best job it can at communicating the true value of the product and encourage word of mouth and other testimonial evidence to spread the news. Helping customers to see the truth is ultimately the best plan.

Are our sales people acting in the company's best interests?

While companies can look forward to the long term, salesmen on commission with families to support may not. Even while the company wishes to be patient and honest, it may find it hard to control the behaviour of managers whose remuneration is tied to short-term performance.

Tactics to influence customers

Now that you have been warned against using influence tactics, let's have a look at the kinds of tactics available to the unscrupulous seller. After all, if our product really is going to deliver the goods to customers, surely it can't hurt to know what techniques exist to convince customers to buy it?

Advertisers appear to assume that their ads will create a desire for a product the customer would not otherwise want. There are many theories on subliminal influence that advertisers hope will allow them to influence people's choices. Fortunately for all of us, advertising is spectacularly unsuccessful at this.

But one example of how advertising *can* successfully influence purchase decisions is to focus attention on one product feature over another. People tend to find it difficult to trade-off different attributes of a product – how do you decide whether it is better to have a faster computer processor or greater software compatibility in a new PC? Obviously it's best to have both, but if you have to make a trade-off, which do you choose? The problem is that it depends on what exactly you are going to need the product for. By focusing your attention on one kind of need, it is possible to influence your decision.

For example, an iMac ad may remind you of when you use your computer to edit pictures and use the Internet – demanding higher performance and user-friendly software – and play down the need for exchanging files, which favours the ubiquitous Wintel PCs.

It isn't surprising that this works. We tend to rely on stories to help us predict the future. By providing a favourable future story, the company can influence your expectations.

All of the best influence tactics take advantage of weaknesses in the way people make decisions. Ideally, everyone would systematically collect all the available information, identify their decision criteria, rationally analyse the options and make the choice that provides the

Smart things to say

You can't *make* someone choose to buy your products if it's not in their interests.

Smart answers to tough questions

Q: How can companies exploit customers' decision-making short cuts?[1]

A: 'Human exploiters … learn … how to profit from our tendency to respond mechanically.'

Robert Cialdini from *Influence – The Psychology of Persuasion*

greatest value. Frankly, most people can't be bothered. And fortunately there are some pretty effective short cuts. But they can leave customers open to influence.

	Short cut	Exploitation method	Examples
#1	What's popular is good	Show reasonable people who have made the decision. Quote the number of people.	McDonald's 4 billion people served
#2	Generosity should be repaid	Give a small 'free' gift before requesting customers to buy	'Free' sweets in exchange for 'voluntary' charitable donations
#3	Trust an expert	Use authority figures to get your message across	Nine out of ten dentists recommend Colgate
#4	What's in short supply is valuable	Limited-time offers, deliberate supply shortages	De Beers' diamonds, Beanie Babies
#5	Be consistent with previous decisions	Get customers to commit to something small and sell them something large consistent with their previous decision.	Free gifts of products prominently bearing the company's logo. Special offers to new customers.
#6	Expensive is better	Raise prices	Stella Artois beer – 'reassuringly expensive'
#7	More pleasant is more trustworthy	Be nice. Pay attention to décor and comfort	McDonald's excellent bathroom hygiene

Smart quotes

'We are immune to advertising. Just forget it.'

Rick Levine *et al.*
The Cluetrain Manifesto

How to advertise to a cynical public

Of course, advertising is still advertising. People brought up in the modern world tend to have learned to shut out most advertising messages. Advertising is so obviously one-sided it is not generally trusted. So advertising appears to be losing its effect – companies are spending more and more on advertising, but their money is having less and less impact. There's just too much clutter and too many self-serving voices.

Companies are increasingly trying new ways to get their messages across, and new advertising contexts to which we have less immunity. Increasingly this is pushing advertising into our social and cultural world. One example is the use of product placement in movies.

From time to time, advertisers use irony to try to identify with jaded audiences and shock them into awareness. 7-Up's recent advertising campaign 'It's all about the drink' parodies the disingenuous techniques advertisers use to sell their wares. But will consumers become cynical of cynicism too?

The selling power of social networks

The most effective salesman is not even paid by the company. An independent authority the customer already trusts (a doctor or a friend) is the ultimate company salesman. There is no apparent self-interest – a fact that makes their selling message far more powerful.

Companies focus a lot of attention on pleasing small opinion-leading segments because of the impact they have on the rest of the market. Their testimony is the most powerful influence the company can exert. In the PC industry, the adverts are full of incomprehensible references to GHz and USB ports, when the users are predominantly families and office workers. But if the geeks love Dell laptops, the business executive can be sure he is buying the best.

Similarly, fashion houses put a lot of effort into outlandish, super-expensive, hand-made creations that can only be worn by impossibly thin, attractive models who could make a garbage bag look good. But if Cosmopolitan magazine features a designer's catwalk creations, then that designer's off-the-shelf designs are going to be in fashion too.

Companies also hope to tap into word of mouth. Companies use unusual promotions and PR to try to give people a reason to talk about their product with their friends. Of course, companies can't always control what is being said.

Examples of this 'guerrilla marketing' are becoming more common. One music company paid street graffiti artists to spray the name of a new rock band around a city. Some fashion companies are happy to give away expensive products to opinion leaders who become walking testimonials to their brands.

Tupperware parties are an interesting variation. By having people sell products to friends, existing loyalties and trust can be used to provide a strong selling influence in a low-key setting.

Equally powerful are discussion forums and Internet peer-review sites that offer independent opinion from other buyers, rather than the self-serving views of the seller.

The value of having customers who find their own information

An even more powerful salesman is the customer herself. People have a far greater level of trust in information they find for themselves than in information given to them. This is true even when they get that information from the company. A customer who requests information is halfway to purchasing something.

Our best sales people are our customers.

Today the Internet is an important marketing tool for companies. The technology drastically reduces the effort involved for customers to obtain the information they require to make an informed decision. Companies should therefore pay careful attention to their Internet presence – few products may be sold over the Internet, but research reveals that it is already a very important factor in many purchases. Research by JD Power and Associates indicates that in 2000, more than 50% of new car buyers in the US got information from the Internet while choosing which car to buy.

Killer questions

Are we making it easy for customers to sell our products to themselves?

Customers who ask to be sold to – permission marketing

Another approach to getting customers to be open to a company's selling message is 'permission marketing'. The customer accepts advertising they know will be targeted to their interests. No more mailings from credit card companies to the 8-year-old child of the family. Advertising will actually be wanted because it is informative and relevant to decisions the customer is currently making. In exchange, customers provide the company with information and feedback to help the company understand their needs better.

More companies are trying to convince their customers of the benefits of close relationships based on permission marketing. If they can demonstrate that they really can predict what you want to know about, when you want to know about it, they might just succeed.

Customers need reassurance

Once a customer has made a purchase, particularly a large one, resentment can still develop if the customer is uncertain that they've made the correct decision. Because of the importance of repeat purchasing, many companies put a good deal of effort into reassuring their customers that they have made the correct decision.

A study of car advertising found that advertising played a more important role in reassuring existing customers that they had made the correct choice than in influencing new customers' decisions.

Summary of main points

- As much as companies would like to influence their customers' decision-making process, they cannot alter people's needs in any fundamental way.

- The best they can do is to draw attention to particular needs at the right time.

- In the short-term, it is possible to influence customers' decisions. But if influence is used to sell products that do not ultimately provide long-term value, the customer will resent it and the company will lose out financially in the long term.

- It is therefore best to focus on helping the customer to come to an informed decision that is in their long-term best interest, and reassuring them their decision was correct.

Notes

1   Based on Robert Cialdani's *Influence: The Psychology of Persuasion*

7 Efficiency Gains from Technology Investment

Why technology is efficient

Time now to leave the world of the customer and head to the factory for a closer look at how companies can produce products *efficiently*.

As you will recall from Chapter 3, 'How do Companies Create Value?', the main way companies become more efficient is by investing in technology.

The benefits of investing in technology come through two different processes:

- investing in new technologies that allow us to do more with less; and

- learning to use technologies more efficiently.

The distinction between technology and learning is, in reality, rather blurred. But separating the two ideas allows us to see more clearly the strategies companies adopt to become more efficient.

This chapter focuses on finding and investing in new 'big ideas' that can make a dramatic difference to productivity. Efficiency improvements through learning will be looked at in detail in Chapter 8, 'Learning How to be More Efficient'.

Smart quotes

'The quantity of industry increases in every country with the increase of the stock [capital].'

Adam Smith, *The Wealth of Nations*

The economics of investing

As we saw in Chapter 3, 'How do Companies Create Value?', technologies are new ways to create more value with less effort and resources. But new technology radically alters the economics of a business because it usually requires a large up-front capital investment for machines, training, systems etc. in order to achieve lower per-unit costs. As a result, it pays to do things on a large scale.

The fact that new technologies require large capital costs has three economic impacts on the business:

- *Rate of return* – the bigger the investment required, the bigger the reduction in per-unit costs needs to be to justify it.

- *Barriers to entry* – the bigger the investment required to operate in an industry, the harder it is to enter the market.

- *Commitment* – the bigger the investment required, the less flexibility you have in changing strategy down the track.

Smart quotes

'Civilization advances by extending the number of operations we can perform without thinking about them.'

Alfred North Whitehead

Economic impact of capital: what rate of return do investors need?

How can we know how much reduction in per-unit costs we need to justify a given investment?

The main consideration is the cost of borrowing money. In order for an investment to be worthwhile, the performance improvement must give you enough additional profit each year to cover the interest payments and repay the loan.

As we shall see later (Chapter 16, 'Keeping Track of the Money') the cost of borrowing for a company is typically somewhat higher than merely the rate of interest on a bank loan, but the idea is the same.

Typically, investments are judged according to their 'rate of return'. This is the average additional profit as a percentage of the amount invested. Invest $100 to get back $10 each year and the rate of return is 10%.[1]

So long as the rate of return is higher than the cost of borrowing, the investment is worth making.

Smart people ot have on your side: Warren Buffet – smart investor

Warren Buffet invests through his company, Berkshire Hathaway. It's a public company, so anyone can benefit from Warren Buffet's investing skills. Over the past 35 years Berkshire Hathaway has made an annual 23% rate of return. So what's the secret of Buffet's success? According to him, it's all about looking at industries he understands, finding undervalued opportunities and unlocking their hidden potential. If Buffet doesn't think he can get performance well above the stock market average rate of return, he doesn't invest.

Economic impact of capital: how investments prevent competitors from entering the industry

In most industries, a company needs to invest heavily in state-of-the art technology in order to compete. If there are already other competitors in the industry, you need to be certain that you'll be able to compete effectively against them to earn a decent return on the investment.

One of the reasons that new competitors cannot compete on equal terms is that it takes time to learn how to use a new technology efficiently (see Chapter 8, 'Learning How to be More Efficient'). So if you are late to enter a market, you have a whole lot of catching up to do. The more competitive the industry, the more catching up you need to do.

A second reason high-investment-cost industries are hard to enter is that entering a market requires the entrant to add a significant amount of new capacity to the industry. Only by entering with plenty of capacity do you have a hope of matching competitors' costs (high investment means that it's cheaper to produce on a *large scale*). But adding this much additional supply to an industry may drive prices down so low that the expected return cannot justify the investment. No thoughtful new entrant would enter an industry when doing so destroys any chance of making a profit from it.

Economic impact of capital: investments commit you to a strategy

New entrants do have one thing in their favour. They can start with the newest, most efficient technologies, while competitors are still lumbered with older technologies they're still paying off.

The problem with investing in a capital-intensive technology is that you're locked-in to using that technology for a long period of time.

If you try to replace your existing technology with something newer, you incur all the capital costs all over again and further increase your debts. Given the choice, your cheapest option is to stick with your existing technology.

In general, the more capital you invest, the less flexibility you have.

Investment in working capital

Not all investments take the form of machines. Investments also include other situations where an up-front cost is needed to gain future performance improvements.

An example is working capital. Working capital reflects the cost of doing business. In almost all businesses, you spend cash acquiring materials and labour long before you receive anything back from your customers. This means that you have to invest a large sum of money in a business in simply getting it up and running. (Working capital is dealt with in more detail in Chapter 16, 'Keeping Track of the Money'.)

Ideas are easy to copy

Although implementing most technologies requires investment, the ideas themselves are free. It might require research, creative thought and expertise to come up with a new idea. But once an idea is hatched, anyone can copy it with relatively very little effort.

Ideas are free.

In most industries technological secrets are hard to keep. So technology is not the most secure competitive advantage unless it can be backed up by a more tangible advantage.

The problem can be seen clearly in the pharmaceutical industry. A new drug often takes ten years and tens of millions of dollars to develop.

But a competitor can produce a generic version for a fraction of the cost and effort.

So why would any company bother to develop a new drug? Governments tend to take a pragmatic approach – drugs are a benefit to the community as a whole, so it is worth providing drug companies with an incentive to develop them. The usual method is to issue patents, which give developers a monopoly for up to 20 years to earn back their investments. (In practice more than half of this time is taken up with testing and product development, so a drug patent usually has less than ten years to earn back its development costs.)

Companies need to be on the look out for ideas from outside their company that might help improve their productivity. Just because an idea doesn't cost money to acquire, or isn't protected by patents, it doesn't mean it isn't valuable. The best thing about ideas is they cost nothing to copy.

But such free ideas don't sit easily with the market economy. If they can simply be copied by anyone, where is the incentive to produce them, package them, promote them or help people use them?

The Linux operating system is an interesting case in point – it was developed largely over the Internet by a community of altruistic volunteers for the benefit of everyone. No one makes money from Linux, so it is genuinely remarkable that it was developed at all.[2] For most programmers who worked on it, the only reward was kudos and hopes of an end to Microsoft's monopoly.

The Internet is also the home of other similarly altruistic attempts to share ideas such as Project Gutenburg – a free online library.

But the biggest initiatives in idea-spreading come from governments keen to help the economy grow by using as many ideas as possible. Universities and schools are *all* about giving people access to free ideas for the benefit of all.

How to promote technological innovation

Technology can still be a source of competitive advantage. But the ease of copying ideas means that companies looking to win advantage through innovation must be able to come up with new ideas on a regular basis.

Many companies search hard for the right ingredients for technological innovation. Some of the best innovators include AT&T, IBM and Xerox, all of which have research departments (Bell Labs, IBM Research Centre and Xerox PARC respectively) that have come up with some of the most original and influential technological ideas in recent times. Where these centres of development succeed is by encouraging smart people to follow their smart ideas even if there is no immediate pay-off for their parent companies.

It's not enough to have good ideas – we need to turn them into great products.

While these research centres are much envied, they are hardly examples of great business. They are very expensive to run and fund. Moreover, their companies have not always been the primary beneficiaries of the great ideas they have produced. Tellingly, Xerox made nothing of its development of the Windows/Icons/Mouse/Pointer (WIMP) computer interface, which was eventually developed by Apple, and copied by Microsoft, who has been the biggest winner of all.

A better example is to be found again in the pharmaceutical industry where the need to create new breakthroughs is much more urgent. Many companies have systematic approaches to finding new drugs.

Smart quotes

'The best way to have a good idea is to have lots of ideas.'

Linus Pauling, Scientist

But drug development is still a frighteningly hit-and-miss affair and extremely costly. As often as not, new drugs come from small companies who license them to larger companies to produce and distribute them.

Some companies seem to do better than others at innovation. But it is clear that no one has found a perfect system for producing ideas on demand. It seems they can come from anywhere and for obscure reasons.

Some systematic processes for development may help. Many companies have tried to use lateral thinking and related techniques to help produce original ideas, occasionally successfully.

A good example of the way great ideas can occur is the development of Post-It Notes. Post-It Notes developed from a happy accident. A technician developed an adhesive that wouldn't set. But rather than abandon it as another failure, a little creativity suggested a use – sticking down paper temporarily. 3M's remarkable success with Post-Its, filling a customer need most customers didn't even know they had, is a symbol of the creative process – experiment, lucky accidents and a keenness to see opportunity everywhere.

Smart things to say

Great ideas can come from anywhere. We need to cast the net as wide as possible and offer rewards for them.

Smart people to have on your side: Rosabeth Moss Kanter

Innovative ideas can come from anywhere
'Innovation is always a surprise. By definition it is something no one has thought of before ... Creative new possibilities can emerge in any field, in any industry.'

For Moss Kanter, innovation requires companies to spread the net wide, open up to ideas from unfamiliar places and, most importantly, destroy the barriers to communication and initiative that often stifle innovative ideas and prevent them from being put into action. By developing a culture supportive of innovation, even large companies can become innovative. Or, as Moss Kanter would say: even giants can learn to dance.

Smart people to have on your side: Edward De Bono

Creative thinking
De Bono's ideas on creative thinking (see Chapter 4, 'How to Meet Customers' Needs') have become particularly prominent in recent years as companies place increasing emphasis on innovation. Companies using De Bono's ideas to aid innovation include IBM and Du Pont.

The battle between innovators and 'fast followers'

So a strategy of constant innovation suffers from three problems:

- it is unreliable;

- it is expensive; and

- its gains are usually short-lived.

Moreover, many industries are dominated not by the original innovators, but by fast followers – companies who come in later, pick up the idea and make it successful.

Often, by starting out after the early trial-and-error days, a fast follower can use the pioneer's experience to avoid pitfalls, save a lot of development effort and improve on the idea. As a result, their investment costs are much lower.

Can we afford the cost of innovation?

Can we afford the cost of not innovating?

This is clearly an egregious example of getting a free ride on the back of someone else's ideas! Where is the incentive to improve if others get all the spoils from your hard work?

Early developers may not always become the eventual market winners, but they can do pretty well because at least at the start there is relatively little competition. While Apple didn't dominate the PC market despite it's revolutionary use of the WIMP interface in its Macintosh computer, it did claim a decent market early, made good money and was very successful for a while. In essence it claimed a 'finder's fee' for its idea, even if it didn't get as much from the idea as Microsoft.

There may be many reasons why innovative companies do not always dominate the markets they create. Companies that are great at innovating are not necessarily good at running a business in the long-term: the cultural requirements are very different. Innovators may also be less ready to accept ideas from outside their own company, while followers are necessarily more open.

Why do all the hard work, when someone else will do it for you?

Besides, being a fast-follower is not so easy. Being late into a market can be fatal if the early leader does their job well. You generally need a significant value benefit to win market share from an incumbent, so just following isn't enough: you still need to find a big competitive advantage. Being a latecomer often means that many of the limited resources are already tied up – e.g. skilled employees and distribution channels – so that it is costly to get access to them. And the cost of learning can be high.

And while fast followers often come to do better from the market than pioneers, it is not clear that fast following is an effective strategy. For one innovator, there may be several prospective 'fast followers'. Of these, only one may have the necessary luck and skill to be successful. So although a fast follower comes to lead the industry, it may prove more a miss than a hit strategy. It may not be nice to see another benefit from your innovations, but innovating may be the better strategy for those who are good at it.

Conversely, if you miss out on a big new idea and wish to become a fast follower, it would be wise to ensure you have a strong operational advantage to back up your fast-follower strategy.

The importance of 'core competence' in innovation

Core competence is an idea we will pursue in more detail in the next chapter, but it bears consideration here too.

Core competence is what allows a company to compete profitably in an industry. It is the accumulation of specific technologies, processes, knowledge and experience in the company. If you want to compete in the industry, you must have the right competencies.

The classic example is Canon's core competencies in fine optics, precision mechanics and microelectronics that allow it to compete successfully in many related fields such as fax machines, scanners, cameras, fibre-optic switches etc.

Having core competencies in the critical industry technologies is usually a prerequisite for innovation.

In many industries, a core competence spans many different technologies. To compete in fax machines for example, you need to know about paper-feeding, data-manipulation and how to read information from paper. The combination of these areas of expertise can lead to novel combinations – such as new kinds of bar codes. The more areas of technology you have expertise in, the more opportunities there are for finding novel combinations. So developing core competencies is also a way to develop opportunities for innovation.

Summary of main points

- A technology is a big idea that allows you to create more customer value more efficiently.

- Most technologies require substantial investment, which is only worthwhile if the resulting productivity improvement outweighs the cost of the investment.

- Large investments are a double-edged sword – they allow efficiencies and reduce competition, but they can also limit flexibility.

- Technology breakthroughs can create an important competitive advantage, but companies hoping to succeed as innovators must:

- learn to innovate efficiently;
- produce lots of ideas;
- be open to ideas from unusual sources, and to develop their ideas effectively and quickly.

Notes

1 Very uneven returns can be expressed as a single number rate of return, although the mathematical procedure is rather more complicated than simply averaging annual profits. The actual method puts more weight on cash received sooner rather than later.

2 Some companies, such as Red Hat, try to make money by providing support to Linux users, but Linux's developers do not receive any royalties.

8 Learning How to be More Efficient

How learning improves efficiency

Big ideas are all very well, but they are not enough to be efficient. MBA students may know all the theories, but that doesn't automatically make them great managers. (According to one joke, MBAs are virgins who've memorized the *Kama Sutra*.)

Similarly, much of the efficiency gains associated with new technologies only come when they are put into practice. Only by *doing* can you discover the minor problems that plague implementation, and find those important tips that keep everything running more smoothly. It may be discovered that a machine tends to jam, but that blowing air through it to clear dust can substantially reduce stoppages. When the bottom line is what matters, that can be just as important as finding the right machine for the job.

The experience curve (see Fig. 8.1) shows that as companies gain experience their costs fall.

Focus on quality not costs

While looking at manufacturing costs is instructive, we would be better off looking at a wider measure of the improvements we can get from learning. Learning can also help us improve customer value.

Smart answers to tough questions

Q: How does learning affect costs?

A: The phenomenon of learning is well documented. Several studies have shown that as companies gain more experience, their costs fall. In one of the earliest studies, Boston Consulting Group found that the cost of producing integrated circuits reduced by 25% on each doubling of experience. Further studies have shown that this pattern is common in many manufacturing industries with 20–30% reductions in costs being seen for each doubling of volumes. Similar learning effects have also been shown in service industries. The 'experience curve' offers a big efficiency advantage to those that start early and produce in large volumes.

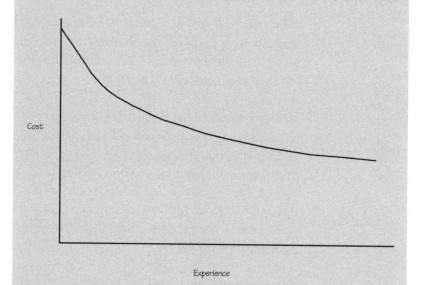

Fig. 8.1 The experience curve.

The best approach to overall improvement comes from focusing on quality rather than cost. By focusing on quality, you can provide more value to customers *and* lower manufacturing costs!

Smart things to know: Six Sigma

Motorola's policy on production errors – Six Sigma is a statistical measure that means 3.4 defects per million i.e. 99.9997% accuracy.

Quality, when applied to manufacturing, means that processes operate to a higher degree of accuracy. Instead of producing a part to within 0.1mm of what was specified, you attempt to manufacture to within 0.001mm.

Prevention is cheaper than cure.

The primary benefit is fewer production problems and stoppages, which are usually caused by variances in materials and activities – reduce the variances and many of the problems disappear. The savings can be enormous. If a single manufacturing process has to be stopped for an hour, nothing can be produced and often problems accumulate elsewhere in the company. Meanwhile, many fixed costs – especially people and facilities costs – are still ticking over. The firefighting effort to get everything running again also uses up valuable management time. A few stoppages like that and months of profits can be destroyed.

High quality manufacturing also translates to better customer value. Consistent accuracy means that customers face fewer variance-related problems and costs too.

Many companies have demonstrated that a focus on quality manufacturing pays off.

Quality in non-manufacturing industries

Quality also applies outside the manufacturing industry. Even services can benefit from reducing the causes of their problems. Perhaps poor filing practices in an insurance company create a lot of additional work in hunting down policy documents. Applying more accurate processes would reduce problems and costs and improve customer satisfaction.

How to descend the experience curve faster

So quality is a better measure of our progress down the experience curve than costs. But how can companies increase the rate at which they get learning-related benefits?

Two methods have been demonstrated to speed up learning.

The first method is to increase the rate at which new knowledge is shared and incorporated into standard procedures. When new techniques are found, managers are responsible for spreading the ideas to other people.

For example, in a major retail bank, there was a big drive to try to package home insurance with home loans, but success rates were low. In principle it was a great deal for customers, but loan arrangers had problems communicating this information. Managers noticed that one arranger had a very high success rate. Immediately he was asked to go round to other bank branches to share his insights with other arrangers. Within six months, the success rate increased from less than 20% to over 60%. The insurance division's profits doubled as a result.

The second method is to increase the rate at which new ideas are tried. In companies that encourage experimentation, learning is much faster especially during the critical early period with a new technology. Small teams tend to learn more quickly than large, hierarchical organizations, because everyone can take responsibility for improvement (we will look at teams again in Chapter 14, 'Designing an Effective Organization').

Smart things to say

Often the biggest gains come not from the big new ideas, but from learning how to apply existing ideas better.

Smart people to have on your side: Edgar Schein

The learning organization
Schein is an organizational psychologist. His interests lie primarily in how organizations create culture and how they learn. For Schein, one of the most important factors in creating a learning organization is to provide people with 'safe havens': opportunities to practise, support for taking risks, encouragement for learning, and rewards for contributions.

How quality management can improve learning

Quality management is a systematic approach to improving learning that focuses on improvements in quality. It works to identify and fix the causes of quality problems one by one. It focuses on the biggest problems first so that the greatest benefits come as quickly as possible. The process is continuous so that once large problems are solved, it is time to move on to smaller problems until the process cannot be improved any further cost-effectively. The big gains come early, but can lead to a lasting advantage over the competition.

Smart answers to tough questions

Q: How can companies use quality management to learn faster?

A: GE's quality programme consists of four phases:

1 *Measure* the variances of processes that contribute to errors.
2 *Analyse* the root causes of problems and explain why they are causing defects.
3 *Improve* performance by finding possible solutions, quantifying their costs/benefits and designing a plan for implementing the most rewarding.
4 *Control* the ongoing improvements through monitoring, and institutionalize changes through procedures, feedback and training to ensure that the new processes meet desired performance standards.

> **Smart quotes**
>
> 'My only regret is that I didn't come across this [quality management] sooner.'
>
> Jack Welch, Former CEO of GE

Using quality management outside the factory

The quality management approach can be adapted to a wide range of processes including in service industries.

Managers can use it as a template for improving any company's ability to efficiently create customer value. By systematically searching for the biggest sources of potential improvement and finding solutions to them, management can rapidly improve the company as a whole.

> **Smart people to have on your side: W Edwards Deming**
>
> *Quality guru*
> The 'quality' revolution is widely seen as a Japanese phenomenon – in the 1970s, Western companies were made acutely aware of their inefficiencies by highly efficient Japanese competitors who used quality management techniques.
>
> Ironically, the quality movement started in the US. Deming was a statistician working at the US Census Bureau who was interested in applying statistical techniques to improve efficiency. His ideas received little support in the US, but were taken up enthusiastically in 1950s Japan, fanatical about 'catching up' with the West. Over the next 20 years, quality gurus and Japanese managers refined Deming's original ideas and developed techniques to apply them. The success of Japanese manufacturers in the 1970s immediately led to an enthusiastic adoption of quality management in the West and the rise of new quality gurus. But even today's quality management ideas are strongly based on Deming's original ideas.

Smart people to have on your side: Gary Hamel and C.K. Prahalad

Core competence
Core competence emerged as a strategically important issue following a highly influential article by Hamel and Prahalad[1] that examined why some Japanese manufacturers had outperformed their US competitors. They concluded that the reason was strategic rather than operational. The Japanese companies deliberately focused on developing a set of core competencies. Their ability to share competencies between businesses allowed them to develop a greater level of expertise, improve innovation and generate new opportunities by cross-fertilizing ideas. Hamel and Prahalad believed that the principal obstacle to US companies adopting a similar strategy was organizational – the divisionalized form of many US companies made it hard to share competencies between businesses.

'Obviously, diversified corporations have a portfolio of products and a portfolio of businesses. But we believe in a view of the company as a portfolio of competencies as well.'

Using learning for competitive advantage – 'core competence'

'Core competence' is about using learning to create a competitive advantage. Core competence is the set of skills a company has that allow it to compete profitably in an industry.

It would be nice to be the best at every skill required in an industry, but in reality it is neither practical nor necessary to do so. So long as performance meets the industry standard across the board, it is enough to have a core competence (that is a set of industry-leading skills) in just one critical part of the value chain. In competing in the building products industry, for example, a competitive advantage can be built on being significantly better at managing customer logistics.

To constitute a valuable core competence, a skill must be:

- a very valuable part of the value chain; and

- performed better than by anyone else in the industry.

Core competence leads to an operational advantage in an industry, but perhaps more importantly from a strategic point of view, a core competence can be leveraged. An industry-leading critical skill in one industry can be used to compete in other industries in which this skill is also important. If your company competes in several industries with similar core competencies, combining knowledge and skills across businesses can improve efficiency in all of them.

A core competence can be tough for competitors to copy since it often consists of a complex mixture of complementary technologies, production skills and cultural traits. So core competence can provide a long-term competitive advantage.

A core competence also ensures that the company can continue to compete in the future because, while technology can always be bought-in or subcontracted, new developments and innovation require industry-leading in-house expertise. It is all too easy for companies to 'hollow themselves out' through sub-contracting only to discover they are unable to compete as technology develops.

How do you develop a core competence?

The first step to developing a core competence is to identify critical skills in which to excel. These must be the most critical parts of the value chain or the most critical technologies in an industry. It helps if you can find a skill critical in more than one of your businesses.

Management time can then be put into development of learning and knowledge sharing in these areas to develop them to an industry-leading standard. In large companies, this often means taking isolated pockets of experience out of the various operating divisions and combining them into a separate unit, or at least greatly improving communications between divisions.

The fastest approach to developing a core competence is to use one that is already developed. Companies frequently use alliances and acquisitions to fast track their development of critical skills.

Using core competence in practice

There are generally two problems with using core competence in practice:

- identifying what your core competence is; and

- determining whether the core competence can be applied to another industry.

It's not a useful core competence unless it results in superior performance.

A large number of companies proudly proclaim their core competencies as 'mass manufacture of small items', 'managing customer accounts', 'high quality engineering' etc., but then they ask why they are not performing at the top of their industry. Clearly, although they have accumulated a great number of difficult skills, these are not sufficient to be useful core competencies.

Furthermore, successful companies struggle to work out what exactly made them successful in their own industry in the first place, let alone trying to work out whether these skills can be applied in another industry.

To illustrate, a major rubber products manufacturer felt that its success was due to a core competence in 'high quality, high volume, low value production'. And on that basis, they invested heavily in the food industry, which also appeared to require 'high quality, high volume, low value production'. But was there actually any real overlap in critical skills? The new business was a disaster. Clearly the skills were not the same, but how could they have known?

The only way to tell for sure is to get to know what these core competencies look like on the factory floor. Are the skilled people in one industry able to talk in the same terms to people in the other? Are the problems they face similar? Are the kinds of solutions they find similar?

'High quality' can mean getting product mixtures within very tight tolerances in rubber products manufacture, but can mean 'very high standards of cleanliness' in food products, for example. The company struggled to come to terms with the differences in culture and procedures needed to adjust.

So what about Canon, one of Hamel and Prahalad's case studies of core competence? Is their skill in 'fine optics, precision mechanics and microelectronics' really at the cutting edge and is it really what drives their success? Certainly Canon has a group of technicians skilled in many technologies, although only a few are really at the cutting edge. Perhaps more importantly, they have a group of people with experience of solving practical problems and an organization conducive to cross-divisional cooperation, innovation and knowledge sharing.

But these too constitute a form of core competence. Core competence doesn't have to be solely technological – it can be any important business process that is critical to success and which the company has learned to perform so well that it provides a competitive advantage. Innovation, design and product management are all areas in which core competence can be attained.

Actually identifying what makes a company successful at what it does – i.e. what its core competencies are – is so difficult that different peo-

Killer questions

Do we have a core competence that gives us superior performance in our industry? Can we use it successfully in other industries?

ple are likely to come to very different conclusions. Developing and transferring a core competence to a new industry is always therefore risky, but if the people talk the same, do similar things and face similar problems, then a core competence could well be transferable.

So, in practice, how useful is the idea of core competence?

In aiming to develop core competencies companies must combine and share knowledge and skills – and that alone is likely to have positive consequences.

How to manage organizational knowledge

Given the importance of learning, it is reasonable to ask how to help share information and expertise within an organization.

The easiest way to maximize the benefit of experience is to create well-defined procedures and rules that encapsulate the practice of the best people in the organization. This way you can be sure that if something worked in one place, it will work in others, even if the people are very different.

But strict rules can be dangerous – change the conditions, or face a new problem and the procedures could lead to the wrong behaviours. Rules work well as a quick way for non-experts to behave like experts in most situations. But at some point, you want to turn your non-experts into experts, so that they can adapt to new situations.

Expertise can be divided into two categories:

- *factual knowledge*, which allows the expert to solve problems; and

- *tacit knowledge*, which cannot easily be written down, including behavioural responses and intuition, which the person may not even be aware of knowing.

It is not always necessary to have factual knowledge. Often it is enough to know where to find it. Do you need to keep in memory the specifications for a certain machine part? Not if you can get hold of the information very quickly.

Computer systems for knowledge management are excellent for storing this kind of knowledge and distributing it around the company.

'Tips and tricks' could also be stored in a computerized knowledge management system, although it is less easy. The number of such learned tricks can be vast, hard to organize effectively, hard to identify as important and consequently very hard for others to make effective use of. Keeping them up to date is also a drain on the experts, not least because they get little benefit from putting things they already know into these systems.

As for experience and learned behaviours, these are all but impossible to put into computer systems, because this kind of knowledge *feels* intuitive. It may be possible to observe experts and try to deduce what they know, but it is an arduous and uncertain process. Even if such rules can be identified, it may be very difficult to instil them in others.

Smart things to say

IT systems provide tools that help companies retain knowledge and help people act more like experts, but they cannot completely replace real experts.

A good portion of the skill and knowledge in a company will always consist of tacit knowledge stored in people's heads and cannot be effectively transferred to systems (at least not until computers can start thinking like people). So what to do?

The first thing is to make sure experts stay in the company. Since they bring your core competence, and hence competitive advantage, to work every day, they are incredibly valuable people. They may not get paid all that much, but their economic value can be huge.

The second thing is to try to train new experts. Let experts work side by side with newer staff to help the newcomers see what they need to learn. Give experts the responsibility to train up other people in their skills – perhaps with a mentoring or apprenticeship system. It may be a severe drain on the experts and the company, but the effort is worthwhile – the company's productivity will always be limited to the productivity of a few people if the knowledge continues to reside in just a few minds.

Where experts can write down or teach what they know, then they should be encouraged to do so. Teaching, especially, can be a great way of identifying what is important to others and what is not. Good note-taking practices might also help others learn or pick up on the work of an expert who, for whatever reason, leaves the company.

Summary of main points

- Learning is a process of gradual improvement – with more experience, costs fall and quality rises.

- Accelerating the learning process and replicating the knowledge of experts is critical to the success of any company.

- Quality management provides a formal way to accelerate learning; and
- Good knowledge management practices are essential for maintaining and sharing learning.

Notes

1 'The Core Competence of the Corporation', C.K. Prahalad and Gary Hamel, *HBR* May–June 1990.

PART II

Good Management

9 How to Manage

What do managers do?

*Called a departmental meeting to plan major initiatives, but was interrupted frequently. Attended to a major operational problem. Received an urgent call for information from head office. Prepared for a meeting with an important customer who's flying in today. My secretary wants to take a holiday during the busiest month of the year. The new IT guy isn't working out – better deal with that. I'm also supposed to look at a tender we're bidding on. It's only lunchtime. Good grief! Am I going to get **anything** productive done today?*

Sound familiar? Well, you're not the only one. A study conducted by Henry Mintzberg found that the average management task lasts for less than nine minutes. Nine minutes! That's not exactly conducive to deep thought.

Meanwhile, management is becoming an ever-costlier burden for companies. Over the years, management costs have exploded as companies have become more complex.

Even stodgily industrial companies like Mercedes-Benz have relatively few 'workers' in the traditional sense, consisting of well under half of company employees.

Smart people to have on your side: Henry Mintzberg

The fragmented manager's day
In 1973 Mintzberg conducted a study on managerial behaviour. Rather than ask how managers *should* use their time, he decided to look at what real managers actually did. The insight was that more than 50% of management tasks last less than nine minutes! The prevailing theory that managers were thoughtful planners was blown out of the water. It was also clear that traditional management training was not properly equipping managers to deal with the realities of their jobs.

In the US in 1950 there were 2 'labourers' for every 'craftsman or foreman' in the US. By 1990 this proportion had fallen to 1.4 and it is still falling rapidly.

Meanwhile the number of managerial and administrative staff in manufacturing companies is growing rapidly – today some 30% of all full-time employees directly employed by heavy manufacturing companies are office-based workers. And if contract specialists and consultants are included, the numbers rise further. In other industries the proportion is far higher.

So making managers more efficient is a high priority for companies. Managers first need to make sure that they spend their time doing what really matters.

The continual flow of small urgent tasks sucks up a lot of management time that could be more productively used in other ways. In organiza-

Smart things to say

Management time is one of the company's most precious resources – don't waste it.

Smart quotes

'Don't let urgent tasks prevent you from doing what's important.'

Stephen Covey, Executive Coach

tions, management time is a precious resource and much of it is being wasted.

But before we rush to a solution, we had better be clear what exactly we expect of managers. If we hope to free up more time, how could it be applied more productively to the organization? Not everyone thinks that the fragmentation of managers' time is a bad thing, so we'll need to consider their arguments too.

And if we are going to bemoan the manager's inability to set time aside for what matters, then we also need to consider whether such a thing is possible. Can managers realistically be set free from the constant stream of petty urgencies that engulf them?

What should managers be doing?

Well, why do we need managers at all?

First, we need managers to provide all the talented people in the company with a clear goal – one, of course, that efficiently creates customer value. Then, managers need to ensure that everyone knows what role they need to play in achieving it and how to coordinate with other people.

Am I spending enough of my time on what really matters?

Let's take a closer look at Drucker's five tasks of management (see box below).

Smart answers to tough questions

Q: What should managers be doing?

A: Peter Drucker translates companies' management needs into five distinct management tasks:

- *Vision*: 'Motivating and communicating'. Set a clear direction for the organization. Unite everyone behind this vision.
- *Planning*: 'Setting objectives'. Detailed planning to articulate the steps the company needs to take to achieve its vision.
- *Organization*: Delegate tasks. Provide an organizational structure to ensure that the plan can be carried out effectively.
- *Monitoring*: Ensure that the organization operates smoothly. Identify obstacles and failures early so that objectives can be refined or the organization altered.
- *Development*: Ensure that the organization continually enhances its capabilities.

Management roles: creating a vision

Vision is all about the big ideas of the organization. What is the organization's main purpose? What basic recipes will we use for efficient customer value creation and staying ahead of the competition? What are the values, priorities and beliefs of the company that will ensure long-term success?

Every group within the company can benefit from its own vision. For a conglomerate, the vision for its head office might be, '… to manage a portfolio of related businesses to create excellent financial returns based on: exploiting synergies between businesses, excellent management and strict financial discipline'. For a particular business within the conglomerate it might be, '… to provide fairly priced office supplies that enhance routine office tasks'. For the management accounting department it might be, '… to add value by providing fast, effective and accurate information so senior managers can make better decisions'.

Each vision should include the following elements:

- a demarcation of which needs of which customers will be served;

- a basic plan for efficiently creating customer value and achieving competitive success; and

- a means of measuring success.

A vision is not forever. The vision is a simplified way to communicate the company's or division's strategy – change the strategy and the vision must change too.

Sometimes it is the other way around: strategy reflects the basic beliefs and values embodied in a corporate vision. For example, Audi's vision: 'Advance through technology' (*Vorsprung durch Technik*) reflects a belief that a strong focus on quality and technological excellence will pay off in terms of customer satisfaction and innovation. The strategy of the company is a reflection of this belief.

Communicating the vision is just as important. If an organization is to coordinate its actions effectively, everyone needs to be working to the same objective. And since people easily lose sight of the purpose of their actions, the corporate vision must be communicated frequently, passionately and in every possible context. If the vision is compelling, it is a great motivator.

Smart quotes

'Through small deeds, accomplish great things.'

Lao Tsu, *Tao Te Ching*

One way to improve communication of the corporate vision is to turn the weakness of a manager's fragmented day into a strength: use the many opportunities to interact with people to communicate the vision and add a little influence to a lot of different projects.

CEOs' jobs consist almost entirely of vision communication. It is the one job so important to the firm as a whole that it cannot be delegated.

Management roles: strategic planning

Planning is a critical task in any organization. The objective is to translate the broad vision into specific initiatives. People need to know what to do. Resources must be allocated. And actions coordinated.

Failing to plan, is planning to fail.

We won't deal here with the details of planning. They are dealt with in Chapter 11, 'Forecasting Market Dynamics', Chapter 12, 'Creating a Lasting Competitive Advantage' and Chapter 13, 'A Systematic Approach to Planning'.

Strategic planning is a difficult and time-consuming process. Good information must be collected and analysed carefully. Deep operational understanding and a degree of creativity are needed to formulate practical actions. Plans must be made for both longer-term initiatives and weekly activities. Usually many busy managers need to find time to collaborate. Managers therefore need to set aside large blocks of uninterrupted time to dedicate to planning.

Management roles: organizing for action

Once a strategy is formulated it needs to be put into action. Complex tasks need to be turned into actions for individuals. Delegation and goal-setting are important managerial skills that we will look at in detail in the next chapter, Chapter 10, 'How to Delegate'.

Often it helps to group people together to get benefits from teamwork, shared knowledge, shared resources and efficient communication, so a structure conducive to these must be created. We will look at the approaches to organization in Chapter 14, 'Designing an Effective Organization'.

A great deal of managers' time is spent organizing. Most is day-to-day task-management. But managers must also pay attention to the design of the organizational structure. This requires focused bursts of uninterrupted time.

Management roles: monitoring performance

Creating strategy and putting it into practice in an organization is all very well. But managers can rarely expect to get everything right first time. Getting feedback is therefore essential. Careful monitoring also allows managers to get early warning of problems. (We will look in more detail at how organizations can provide information to managers on a systematic basis in Chapter 16, 'Keeping Track of the Money'.)

Again, the fragmented manager's day may be turned to advantage. Many managers find that regular contact with people around the organization can help them stay informed; particularly with information rarely transmitted through formal channels: gossip, hearsay, intuitions, anomalies, fears etc. Managers often deliberately add informal contact with people around them to their schedules to help them stay informed (sometimes referred to as 'management by walking about').

Management roles: developing employee skills and organizational capabilities

With so many demands on time, development tends to be the first thing to be put aside. But without some focused attempt to improve the skills of the organization, they are unlikely to improve on their own. Good managers must therefore ensure they put aside time for their own development and the development of others. A good general rule is that around 10% of time should be invested specifically in development. That means managers too.

Chapter 19, 'How to Become a Great Manager' and Chapter 20, 'How to Teach Yourself New Skills' address how managers can develop their own skills and the skills of others.

Smart quotes

'Developing talent is business's most important task – the *sine qua non* of competition in a knowledge economy.'

Peter Drucker

How to be efficient at managing

The view of the world presented by the five tasks of management is very idealistic. In this world, managers should put large blocks of time aside for value-creating initiatives based on the five management tasks.

Realistically we can't completely escape from interruptions and plan our time completely – unexpected things happen. And we often have to juggle several projects at once – each competing for our limited attention. But we can get a lot closer to this ideal if we follow four time-management strategies:

- *the 80:20 rule*: cherry pick;

- *ask the right questions*;

- *an ounce of prevention*: prevent fires, don't fight them; and

- *teach a man to fish*: delegate well and teach autonomy.

Management efficiency: the 80:20 rule

The first strategy for management efficiency is the simplest: do the really important things first.

Set yourself just a few of the biggest goals.

Management tasks, customer profitability and many other phenomena all tend to conform to a similar pattern. As a general rule, 80% of all the value comes from just 20% of all the effort, customers, products etc.

This rule is very useful because it means that by focusing on just the most important 20% of problems, you can deal with 80% of everything that matters. That's a pretty big bang for your 20 cents.

So with management tasks, the trick is to first deal with the 20% of important issues and leave the remaining 80% to fit in around them or to simply disappear.

Many managers do the opposite, getting the small problems 'out of the way' first – but these provide much less value for each minute of

Smart quotes

'The vital few and the trivial many.'

Joseph Juran, Quality Guru

Smart quotes

'20% of your effort will generate 80% of your results.'

Pareto's Principle

management time (16 times less if the 80:20 ratio is accurate). So if you want to get more efficient, focus more attention on a few important issues and less attention on the little things.

Management efficiency: asking the right questions

One of the biggest problems managers face is that they are inundated with information. Management time is easily drained by the need to 'keep up to date'. Managers need to learn how to be more efficient at extracting what they need to know.

The key to getting useful information from the chaos is asking the right questions. Asking a few well-targeted questions is a far more efficient use of time than poring over a 20-page report that might miss key issues.

Before looking at the information/speaking to someone, decide on your questions:

● What am I trying to find out?

● What are the key pieces of information I need to know?

And formulate your questions accordingly.

Once you've got answers to these questions, follow them up by asking yourself:

● Given the answers I received, what do I think is going on?

● What key pieces of information do I need to be certain of this?

Usually this will give you new questions to ask.

Smart quotes

'[I got to the truth] by asking questions, lots of them. I would sit there and I would ask 18,000 questions and I wouldn't leave.'

Jack Welch, former CEO of GE

For example, if you are running a marketing initiative, you primarily want to know if it has made a difference. The key questions are: 'What happened to volumes?' and 'What happened to margins?' If the answers are not what you expected you can delve further. If, for example, the sales increased, but margins fell, it would be natural to test the theory: 'Did we buy volume through discounting?' Your next questions might be: 'Did our discount policy change?' and 'Did total discounts increase as a proportion of sales?'

Even when reading reports, asking the right questions can save time – relevant information can be found quickly and the rest scanned superficially (see box).

Smart answers to tough questions

Q: How do you get information quickly from large quantities of data?

A:
- Be clear about your questions in advance;
- skim the available data with your questions in mind, looking only for data relevant to them; and
- what information do you need to answer your questions that you didn't get? Is it important enough to expend resources on getting it?

Management efficiency: an ounce of prevention is worth a pound of cure

It almost always pays to prevent problems before they occur. We have already seen the value of this in quality manufacturing, but the principle applies equally to management.

Managers tend to be fire-fighting addicts. When your day is already fragmented, emergencies provide a way to do something important in a responsive manner – whatever else, 'something useful was accomplished'.

But managers would do far better to stop problems occurring in the first place. The old proverb applies – an ounce of prevention is worth a pound[1] of cure.

To prevent crises, managers should apply a similar process to the quality management process we discussed in Chapter 8, 'Learning How to be More Efficient':

- *Monitor* – identify and measure recurring problems that require major intervention; identify potential major problems.

- *Analyse* – identify why these problems occur and the cost/benefit of solving them.

- *Improve* – prepare a plan to eliminate the biggest problems.

- *Control* – put in place procedures to prevent recurrence.

> **Smart quotes**
>
> 'Confront the difficult while it is still easy.'
>
> Lao Tsu, *Tao Te Ching*

Management efficiency: give a man a fish and he'll eat for a day, teach a man to fish and he'll eat for a lifetime

Another big drain on management time is caused by the need to supervise other people. Delegating can often be frustrating – it requires so much supervision time. And delegated tasks never seem to be done quite as well as you might have done them.

Ideally delegation should be a tell-and-forget process – you delegate a task and you only hear about it again when it is successfully completed. Of course it never works like that.

Good delegation is about teaching people to become self-sufficient. Ideally, tasks can be deputised to people who have the skills to deal with any problems that might occur. It is worth investing time to develop self-sufficiency amongst your people. In the next chapter, Chapter 10, 'How to delegate', we'll see how to go about it.

Summary of main points

- Managers' time is highly fragmented. But to be productive, managers need to spend more of their time performing five critical tasks:

  - vision setting and communicating;
  - planning actions to achieve the vision;
  - organizing people effectively;
  - monitoring progress; and
  - developing organizational capabilities.

- Managers need to become great *time* managers before they can be great *business* managers. Effective time management strategies are:

  - doing the big things first;
  - asking the right questions;
  - focusing on prevention; and
  - delegating effectively.

Notes

1 For the metrically minded, a pound is 16 ounces.

10 How to Delegate

How to delegate: the MBO approach

Delegating is so important a part of management that a whole chapter of this book is dedicated to it and especially to a technique called 'management by objectives' (MBO).

The idea of management by objectives is to delegate by setting goals. It sounds almost too simple to be worth mentioning, let alone dedicating a whole chapter to. Until, that is, you contrast it with its more commonly encountered alternative: delegation of duties.

It's great when someone comes back to you saying, 'I started to do what you asked, but it wasn't working out as well as you were hoping, so I did something else that achieves the same thing and it worked out just right.' It's just painful when someone comes back saying, 'I did *exactly* what you asked me to do, but you won't like the results.'

The first employee understood the objective of the task; the second was only concerned with performing the duty. It's easy to see which employee is going to require more management effort.

> ### Smart people to have on your side: Rosabeth Moss Kanter
>
> *Empowerment*
> Empowerment is a theme running through much of Rosabeth Moss Kanter's work, whether she's talking about women in the work place, motivation, ability to change, innovation or organizational culture. For Moss Kanter, empowerment is about giving people more control over their working environment so that they can turn good ideas into action. It is about harnessing the collective abilities of everyone in the organization; freeing them from the tyranny of hierarchical constraints and politics. 'Powerlessness corrupts', as she says.
>
> Management gurus are in unprecedented agreement about the benefits of empowerment. Drucker, Peters, Mintzberg and many others agree that greater individual freedom is the key to improved company performance.

The best employees seem to understand this. They are delightfully easy to manage because they take time to identify the objective behind what they have been asked to do.

Great delegators favour the MBO approach too – it allows employees to take the initiative and add their contribution and requires less supervision. Moreover, the manager is not always as competent as their subordinate in the task, so delegation of duties may not even be an option.

MBO can improve motivation too because it hands control to the employee. It can allow people to contribute far more to their organization. It can even help people more easily understand the link between their work and the goals of the organization.

How to make MBO work

So, easy really! To delegate with MBO, just set employees an objective and a deadline and wait for the results. If it sounds too good to be true, it is. Many managers who have tried to apply MBO have found it frustrating, often getting worse results than from the simpler delegation of duties.

What happened to all those supposed benefits? Managers quickly discover that a goal and a deadline are not enough. MBO poorly applied produces poor results. When employees hit problems, the burden of responsibility can lead to stress and ultimately failure. The result: missed deadlines, failed initiatives and unhappy, demotivated people.

So is MBO one of those ideas that are great in theory but crumple in the face of real situations? Fortunately not – MBO works. The benefits are real and significant. But skilful execution is needed.

Where MBO most frequently fails is that managers provide inappropriate goals, in effect setting employees up to fail.

There's no point setting goals that people can't achieve.

The other big problem faced with MBO is that employees need to learn how to become self-reliant – in the meantime, managers must give them the support they need.

How to set appropriate goals

Good goals obey the following two rules:

- they are within the employee's scope of control; and

- they are within the employee's scope of competence.

Goals should be within the employee's scope of control

It's no good allocating a goal to someone if it isn't in their power to make it happen. Many things we would like to happen depend heavily on factors outside our influence. King Canute can order the tide back until he's blue in the face – but it isn't going to happen.

Equally, there's no point telling an airline pilot to improve the airline's profitability because she has no control over critical variables such as marketing and fuel prices. Even the most dedicated pilot isn't going to try to negotiate a new deal with OPEC just to meet her goals.

But she *can* control the speed and altitude of the aircraft – that lets her trade off fuel-burn against journey time. Fuel burn is important for flight costs, while journey time affects both customer satisfaction and airport costs. So a better goal would be one that reflected the economic impact of these two variables.

Even in our improved goal, there are some factors that lie outside the pilot's control. Air traffic control might divert the flight, for example, or a storm might be encountered. But the new goal eliminates as many externalities as is reasonable.

Goals should be within the employee's scope of competence

The employee may be able to control the critical variables, but does she have the right level of skill to meet the goal?

As an example, take a situation in which a marketing manager delegates the task of improving sales in a certain product to a new junior manager. The senior manager may well have enough experience of the market and the product to know what kinds of initiatives might work, but the poor junior may not have a clue. So delegating this task is almost certain to result in failure.

In this situation, most managers would be tempted to fall back on old-fashioned duty-based delegation – providing the junior manager with a detailed set of tasks to perform.

But a better approach would be to provide the junior manager with a basic strategy for accomplishing the goal, since the operational details should be well within the competence of a well-trained marketing professional.

So, a better goal for the junior manager might be: launch a print media advertising campaign that raises awareness by 10% and gives customers a positive, youthful image of the product.

This goal can be tested directly for its success through market research. If it is achieved, then the job is well done, even if other factors mean that product profitability does not rise as a result – a failure of planning rather than execution and the responsibility of the senior manager rather than the junior.

The value of setting contradictory goals

What could be worse than being given a project that has two seemingly contradictory goals? For example, a marketing manager being asked to increase both realized prices and sales volumes at the same time. Which one is more important? How does one decide which to go for?

But setting contradictory goals is one of the most powerful tools available to managers!

Imagine being set just the goal of bringing in more sales. All things being equal, more customers are good for business. But by far the easiest way to increase sales is by discounting, reducing realized prices. In effect all you are doing is trading one off for the other. You might meet your goal, but have you helped the company? If you're lucky you might have found a more profitable balance, but more likely margins will suffer and the company will be worse off.

The alternative is to set contradictory goals. By setting the twin goals of increasing realized prices and sales volumes at the same time, trading off one for the other is not an option. The only way to achieve both is to fundamentally 'shift the value curve' – to provide more customers with more value. The result will inevitably be better for the company.

Contradictory goals are valuable when the easiest option is a straight trade-off. Other examples of contradictory goals are:

- big company efficiency and small company flexibility;

- higher quality and lower cost;

- more carefully considered decisions, made faster; and

- higher customer value at lower prices.

Smart answers to tough questions

Q: How can contradictory goals be used across the whole company?

A: Kaplan and Norton's Balanced Scorecard

The Balanced Scorecard takes the idea of contradictory goals to its logical conclusion. Goals are set for *all* of the major aspects that determine the company's success:

- short-term financial results, *and*
- long-term customer value;
- internal business process efficiency/quality, *and*
- development of employee skills and corporate knowledge/culture.

How to supervise delegated tasks

Ideally delegating with MBO is a 'tell-and-forget' operation. The person doing the task should be completely autonomous. If the goal is controllable and within the person's scope of competence, then they can be expected to perform the task well.

Once again, reality intrudes. Few employees are ready for unsupervised autonomy. A common experience is that work is rushed and deadlines are missed. Occasionally big problems only become apparent at the last minute, having been hidden from the manager.

Before leaving an employee to their own devices, the manager must ensure they:

- have strong project management skills;

- know when to ask for help; and

- will immediately report to the manager problems and issues that will significantly affect the outcome of the project.

Trust is important. The employee needs to trust the manager to help him if asked and not 'shoot the messenger'. The manager needs to trust the employee to be open and honest about problems and to put their full energy into meeting goals.

Trust takes time to develop. There is a strong element of maturity required from both manager and employee. If the manager provides an open and honest working environment, trust can be built fairly quickly. The manager might, for example, openly admit his occasional errors, to send an important signal that nobody's perfect.

In developing the employee's project management skills, the manager must initially work closely with the employee to determine approaches, split up the work and set a timetable for completion of each part of the work.

During the project, the employee must provide regular updates and work with the manager to adjust schedules as circumstances change.

As the employee gets more familiar with the skills of project management, it is enough for the manager to verify that the correct procedure is being followed and to occasionally review progress.

Finally, once sufficient trust is developed, the employee can be expected to complete the work unaided, informing the manager only of significant changes or problems and responding to inquiries from the manager with a brief update summary.

Throughout this process it helps greatly if the employee retains control of the process. The aim is to make the person feel comfortable with responsibility and provide a sense of ownership and control.

Set interim deadlines

Deadlines are a particularly big issue. If correct project planning procedures are followed, then deadlines will be broken down into small, frequent targets. The manager can provide useful external assistance by putting pressure on the employee to meet interim deadlines.

Without interim deadlines, or without the pressure to meet them, work easily slips behind schedule and work is inevitably finished in a last-minute rush that is the hallmark of poor project management.

Setting appropriate deadlines, though, is a skill that requires experience. Initially at least, employees may need help setting the right deadlines.

Smart quotes

'When people feel controlled rather than empowered, they proceed cautiously.'

Rosabeth Moss Kanter

How to set the right rewards

Organizations that make extensive use of MBO face new challenges in rewarding their staff.

Companies traditionally pay people according to the years of experience normally required to perform the duties of a given job – pay is defined by the *job*, not the person doing it. But since MBO eliminates specific duties in favour of objectives, traditional rewards do not make much sense.

One solution is to pay people for the useful skills and experience they can apply to the project in hand. Actually finding a fair way to measure this is not an easy task. But the benefit is that people are rewarded for the value they can contribute. It is up to the organization to use them effectively.

Smart quotes

'You should pay individuals for what they can do that is related to task performance.'

Edward Lawler, Human Resources Professor

A common form of reward is incentive pay. Rewards should be partially dependent on the achievement of outcomes (including team successes). However, there are two considerations:

1   Make rewards dependent on achieving controllable goals. There is little motivational benefit to rewards that depend strongly on uncontrollable factors.

2   Make the rewards small e.g. 10% of total pay. Much more and they can actually be demotivating, since they shift attention from rewarding a job well done to making a judgement of an individual's worth. Furthermore, since it is impossible to make rewards truly objective, there will always be the opportunity to 'game' the reward system, usually to the detriment of the company.

Also remember that money isn't the only factor that motivates people. It may not even be the most important one. Recognition often matters more to people and is a lot cheaper for the company to provide.

Summary of main points

- Management by objectives is a delegation style that consists of setting goals rather than duties. The key challenge is setting the right goals and developing self-sufficiency in employees:

  - goals should be controllable and within the employee's competence;
  - setting contradictory goals forces employees to shift the value curve rather than simply trade off one factor for another; and
  - self-sufficiency comes with trust, maturity and project-management skills and takes time to develop.

- The move from duties to goals requires companies to reassess the way they reward people.

11 Forecasting Market Dynamics

What is 'strategy'?

Strategy is possibly the most overused term in business. It seems to get tagged on to the start of all sorts of words and phrases, making them sound more important and profound. People talk about 'strategic marketing', 'strategic customer relationship management' and 'strategic capabilities management' when what they really mean is marketing, customer service and core competence.

So what on earth *is* strategy?

Strategy is about making *choices* for the long-term. If we never had to make long-term commitments, there would be no need for strategy: we could just do whatever was best when the time came.

But many important decisions companies make involve long-term commitments:

- Choosing whether to pursue short-term profits, or build customer value for the long-term success of the business.

- Making major investments in new technology represents a commitment to that technology and to a given level of capacity. It will be time-consuming and costly to change later.

- Deciding which product features and customer segments to focus on and which to neglect – the need for focus and consistency demands that we choose a position and stick with it for a long period of time.

- Deciding which operational improvement initiatives to pursue and which to drop – limited funds and personnel mean that only a few can be managed effectively at any given time, and resources will remain committed until these are completed.

For example, Chevrolet, a division of General Motors, failed to decide what part of the market it intended to target and found itself producing models ranging from the sporty to the executive, from the luxury to the mass-market. By failing to make a commitment, it faced numerous conflicts and drains on its resources. Was engine research to focus on low cost or high performance? What did the Chevrolet brand mean to people? The resulting conflicts have contributed to sales figures halving since the mid-1980s.

So, failing to make a commitment is often worse than making the wrong one as resources are spread too thinly to be effective and internal conflict is inevitable. In many cases, an inability to make a commitment can lead to missed opportunities – by the time sufficient resources are committed, the chance to enter a new market has passed.

Smart quotes

'The essence of strategy is in choosing what *not* to do.'

Michael Porter

Smart answers to tough questions

Q: What makes a good strategy?

A:
- A clear goal to unite the organization behind.
- Indicates how to make major choices facing the company.
- Provides a broad plan of action specific enough to work to, but flexible enough to be adapted to circumstances.

Given that a company's resources are limited, success often requires effective concentration and coordination. Strategy involves setting clear long-term goals so that each part of the organization knows how it can contribute effectively.

In business, decisions are often made in an environment of uncertainty. The future cannot be forecast clearly enough to make a definitive decision as to what commitments to make. So retaining some flexibility is valuable. Strategy is about choosing what commitments to make now and which to delay. Strategy is about developing broad plans that can be adapted to circumstances as they arise.

Strategy should be distinguished from tactics. Tactics are the many short-term choices and initiatives that a company must take. A company with a clear strategy determines its tactics in order to achieve its strategic goals. For example, a company with a strategy to develop an upmarket wristwatch brand will choose appropriate tactics: price rises, classy product packaging, marketing to high-income earners and distribution through high-end retailers.

Meanwhile, a company without a clear strategy will find itself making its commitments by the accumulation of its tactical choices. Usually the resulting strategy is incoherent and contradictory. So our watchmaker may in one week lower prices to secure a higher market share and product awareness and in the next start a marketing campaign based on the quality of the product. The result is likely to be brand confusion and might unintentionally initiate a destructive price war with competitors.

The most important strategic idea in business is the decision to prioritize efficient customer value creation over short-term profitability. You *could* use influence techniques to persuade customers to buy products they don't really need, but the strategies that work best in the long term are all based on ways to increase efficient customer value creation.

In determining a strategy, there are two factors to consider:

- In which markets should we concentrate our efforts?

- How will we beat the competition in these markets?

In deciding which markets to concentrate efforts in, we are looking for large, profitable opportunities. One approach is to find new ways to meet customer needs as discussed in Chapter 4, 'How to Meet Customers' Needs'. The other is to follow the market dynamics to growing markets that favour profitable business. This chapter looks at the most important market dynamics and how to predict them.

We will look at how to beat the competition in the next chapter, Chapter 12, 'Creating a Lasting Competitive Advantage'.

The value of getting to new market opportunities first

The enormous advertising expenditures of Internet retailers during 1999 perplexed a lot of people. Companies were spending more than the entire industries' profits on advertising. Normal marketing rules cannot begin to explain this behaviour. The subsequent dot.com collapse seemed to justify the cynics.

Smart quotes

'I skate to where the puck will be, not where it is.'

Wayne Gretzky, Ice Hockey Legend

Where will our profits come from in 5–10 years time?

But actually there was logic to this insanity. Companies were seeking to stake out future profits ahead of time. The Internet will one day dominate retail business (or so it was assumed), so companies should seek to become successful at it ahead of time. When the profits do eventually come, the winners of today's competitive battles will be ideally placed to dominate the lucrative markets in the future.

The opening of a new business frontier allows those who get there first to make great fortunes. It's as if a new gold deposit has been struck and prospectors are heading out to stake their claim on the land right away. There will be plenty of time to dig the mines later.

Smart quotes

'Whoever occupies the battle ground first and awaits the enemy will be at ease.'

Sun Tzu, *The Art of War*

Two critical market dynamics: product lifecycles and macro trends

There are two important long-term market dynamics worth studying to determine new market opportunities. Both have a significant impact on where money can be made and both operate over a sufficiently long time period to allow strategic commitment.

- *Product lifecycles.* New product categories emerge when companies find new ways to meet customers' needs. These product categories tend to follow fairly predictable lifecycles. Some of the stages of the lifecycle are good for profitable business and others bad. As the lifecycle develops, different parts of the value chain are likely to become more favourable than others.

- *Macro trends.* Demographic, economic and behavioural trends tend to take place over long periods of time. Successfully predicting these trends allows you to spot the emergence of new markets and know which markets will grow or decline. Usually a particular market is subject to many different trends. Being able to predict market evolution depends on understanding which trends will dominate.

Market dynamic: product lifecycles

The product lifecycle was originally developed to help companies manage individual products. It was observed that most products follow four distinct stages during their lifecycle and a product in each different stage has different marketing needs (see box).

Of more relevance to corporate strategy, the same four stages are seen in the evolution of *product categories*. While branded products' lifecycles typically last around three years, product categories often last decades. Most new product categories result from the development of new technologies – TV or CD players are good examples. And some product categories can last more or less indefinitely – no one is forecasting an end to the market for concrete.

It is impossible to predict when new product categories are likely to emerge. (But if there is a large customer need, it is a fair bet someone will eventually find a way to meet it.) Once a new product category is established it tends to follow the predictable four-stage pattern.

Phase 1: emergence

Initially many new product categories grow slowly. It takes time for producers to get things right. It also takes time for customers to learn about the new products and what they have to offer. Will the idea take off or will it all fizzle out?

No doubt when Sony's Walkman first went on sale, customers were perplexed as to how it was any benefit to them. But once a few bored commuters began to envy their Walkman-listening peers, there were suddenly reasons to have one. As the price came down and the quality improved, there were no more excuses for not having one.

During the emergence phase, many ideas and companies fail, so risks are high. (What happened to hand-held TVs for example? After a short period of growth, they have all but disappeared.) But for brave pioneers there is a chance that the product will be successful and that they could dominate the future market.

Often product standards are set during this phase that profoundly influence the nature of competitive advantage in future. For consumers it is sometimes entertaining and frustrating to see companies battle over standards for products that don't even exist yet. But what is really being fought over is a huge future market.

Phase 2: rapid growth

The next phase, for those ideas that do take off, is one of explosive growth. Customers catch on. The rate of take-up is limited only by the rate at which new people discover reasons for owning the product.

In this phase, competition is rarely intense and profits are therefore quite high, although growth can require a great deal of investment. Generally this is the easiest time to jump on the bandwagon. Again, market dominance in this phase can be a great opportunity for the future.

Phase 3: maturity

Eventually, growth slows. Sales come from replacements or through selling to more marginal customers as prices continue to fall and quality improves. Demographic and consumer trends might bring some new growth or decline. But on the whole, most customers whose needs can be met are already buying the product.

In maturity, competitive advantage is all-important. Winners can earn good profits since little new investment is needed.

Phase 4: decline

Then, at some stage the inevitable occurs and a new technology, fashion, or need makes the product category obsolete.

Typically in this stage profitability falls rapidly as competitors geared for bigger sales try to maintain volumes. Eventually most competitors drop out of the market during a period of consolidation.

Occasionally enough of a market remains to provide niche opportunities for one or two companies. (There are still companies that make amplifier valves in small quantities, for example, even though transistors have obliterated this once thriving market.)

Bucking the trend – opportunities in declining markets

Most companies in a declining industry retreat from the market, stop innovating and milk what profitable niches remain. But a dynamic innovator can occasionally find an opportunity for growth and high levels of profit.

An interesting example is Nucor Steel. In the 1980s the US steel industry was an archetypal declining market.

There is, and is likely to be for some time, a big market for steel, but the glory days in the US are over. Construction has slowed since the 1950s boom and for many uses, new materials are replacing old-fashioned steel. Meanwhile cheap foreign steel makers have been impinging on the US market. The only chance for competitive advantage seemed to lie in scale – which encouraged excess capacity and price discounting. Overall, the US steel industry was in a pretty pathetic state, with just about every steel maker incurring bad losses.

But against this bleak backdrop Nucor entered the market. Initially it only made steel to provide for its own needs as a steel products fabricator. But by the 1980s while competitors were suffering, Nucor was earning strong profits from steel production and is now one of the biggest steel producers in the US.

Nucor managed this remarkable feat by developing a new technology (an electric-arc furnace process) to produce certain speciality steels for its own use. The new technology proved to be so versatile and efficient that Nucor also found external customers and started building new 'mini mills' to service them. By focusing on particular market segments and products, Nucor has thrived.

How to forecast the product lifecycle

It's one thing to understand the *pattern* of product lifecycles, but quite another to make accurate predictions. Can we go beyond simply describing the product lifecycle and actually forecast when and how big?

Fortunately there is a good analytical model of how the product lifecycle behaves (see box).

The market diffusion model (see box) depends on two main variables:

- *The take-up rate*. This can be estimated from the early stages of growth, or by comparison with similar products. It depends on: the amount of value the product creates for each customer; marketing; and consumer behaviour (e.g. how keen people are to try new gadgets).

- *The eventual market size*. This depends on how many people obtain value from the product. For many products the eventual market size is relatively easy to guess because the market corresponds closely to some easily identifiable group.

Smart answers to tough questions

Q: How can product category lifecycles be forecast?

A: Market diffusion.

The penetration of a new product category into its potential market tends to follow an S-shaped curve. Initially, adoption is slow as only a few people are aware of it. Then the product goes through rapid growth as the existing customer base influences new buyers. Finally, sales begin to slow as the market reaches saturation. Many products show a good fit to mathematical models, which can be used to provide accurate forecasts (see Fig. 11.1).

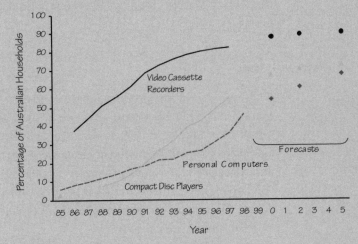

Fig. 11.1 S-shape penetration curves for household technologies

For example, we can use the market diffusion model to forecast the market for Third Generation cellular telephones (those that can run data services similar to the Internet) in the US. The adoption rate can be guessed at by comparison to similar products: the US was relatively slow to adopt cellular phones, but fast to adopt the Internet. 3G phones

Killer questions

How long is the product's lifecycle? Which stage is it in now?

will probably fall somewhere in between. We can test customer attitudes with market research to get a better idea of how rapid adoption is likely to be.

The total market size depends on how many people perceive the product to be of value. Traders and e-mail-dependent executives are likely to benefit initially. Only when prices fall will others follow. Eventually, the market should extend to everyone who currently uses a cellular phone.

The problem with fads

'Fads' are very short product lifecycles that have no maturity phase and a very rapid decline. Usually their growth is motivated by fashion rather than long-term, efficient, customer value creation. Predicting fads is fiendishly difficult, mostly because it can be very hard to tell the difference between a fad and a product category that will persist. Many companies have run into difficulties because they invested heavily during the growth phase of a fad only to be left with worthless stock and unusable spare capacity.

The success of Razor Scooters in 2000 was clearly a fad. But was Internet shopping a fad? Or is it just in temporary decline?

Market dynamic: forecasting market trends

Another important type of market dynamic to understand is market trends. Trends in fashion, population dynamics, customer needs and behaviours all affect market growth over long time periods.

For example, the 'baby boomer' generation[1] has affected many industries as it has aged. In the 1960s and 1970s the music and fashion industries boomed with the dramatic increase in teenagers. By the 1980s, real estate boomed as they bought their own houses. As baby boomers approach retirement age, they are fuelling an investment boom. When they finally retire, they risk putting the pensions system under ruinous strain.

Demographics are very predictable, but other trends are far harder to spot. How do you predict how trends in building styles will change, or whether people will want small or large cars in the future?

First, look for good forecasts by other people who have vested interests – forecasting is a difficult art and usually best done by people who understand the market very well. If, however, there is no acceptable forecast, then it may be necessary to produce your own.

The approach is to break down the trend you wish to forecast into a series of more fundamental contributing trends that *can* be forecast with some accuracy.

Smart answers to tough questions

Q: How can you forecast market trends?

A:
- Determine the fundamental trends affecting the market:
  - examine how these fundamental trends have affected the market in the past and how they ought to affect the market in future.
- Forecast each of these fundamental trends using:
  - expert opinion and published forecasts; and
  - analysis of past behaviour.

- Check that the forecasts are plausible. Do they have controversial implications? Are they consistent with other forecasts?
- Reassemble a forecast of the market from the fundamental trends.
- Compare your forecast with others and try to understand why they are different from yours (be aware of any biases in their forecasts).
- Is my forecast plausible? What are the major implications?
- What level of uncertainty is there in my forecast?

An example of forecasting market trends

A company that manufactures aircraft in-flight entertainment systems might be keen to know how many aircraft will be in service in the future.

First look for existing forecasts. Both Boeing and Airbus provide forecasts for the aircraft market. However they have an incentive to inflate their figures. So we're going to have to generate our own numbers.

The biggest factors influencing aircraft numbers are the growth in passenger traffic and the size of the aircraft. Passenger numbers are quite easy to forecast since they tend to follow a predictable relationship to GDP growth. As large developing countries grow, there should be a big rise in air travel.

The size of planes depends on the types of journeys made – more short journeys means more small planes. It may turn out that most of the new growth is in regional flights, so on average, aircraft will get smaller. So the number of planes will increase.

Armed with a decent forecast, the company can plan a more rapid increase in capacity.

The importance of 'bargaining power' in determining profitability

Product lifecycles and macro trends help companies identify potential opportunities and plan around them. But companies also need to know whether these markets are likely to create profit opportunities for them.

When there is a good business opportunity, the industry value is shared out amongst the industry participants: competitors, suppliers and customers. Who gets how much is determined by the balance of bargaining power between these participants.

Smart people to have on your side: Michael Porter

Five forces
The 'five forces' model is Porter's framework for analysing the attractiveness of industries. Most favourable are those industries that have the greatest bargaining power in their value chain and where there is relatively little competitive pressure.

The *customers'* bargaining power depends on what alternative products (substitute products) are available, on customers' ability to create collective bargaining power, and on the intensity of competition for customers.

The *suppliers'* bargaining power depends on suppliers' ability to concentrate their collective bargaining power and on the importance of their role in the value chain (their value added).

The ability to reduce *competitive pressure* depends on the ways competitors typically compete, opportunities for collusion against other parts of the value chain, and on whether potential entrants can be kept out of the market.

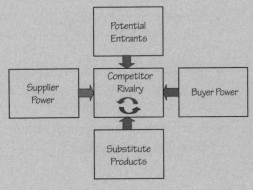

Fig. 11.2 Porter's five forces model of industry attractiveness

What influences bargaining power?

Ownership of critical resources such as technology or customer relationships adds bargaining power. A few large companies generally have more bargaining power over their suppliers and customers than many small companies, because collusion is more likely and because a threat by a large company to withdraw business is more powerful than a similar threat by a small company.

Bargaining power dynamics even extend to the consumer. Consumers' bargaining power depends on what substitutes are available for meeting their needs. It also depends on whether providers can be played off against one another. Government consumer protection also increases consumers bargaining power against companies.

Being able to predict how the bargaining power in a market will evolve is an important factor in determining who will make the money.

How bargaining power alters during the product lifecycle

During the *emergence and growth phase* of the product lifecycle, opportunities for profitability for sellers tend to be quite good:

- there is little competitive rivalry as companies are trying to cope with growth rather than competing for market share;

- customers tend to find it hard to exert much power owing to the low level of competition and the lack of distribution infrastructure;

- if the product category is revolutionary, there may be no effective substitute products; and

- the market tends to be dominated by providers who engage in most of the value chain themselves as there is as yet little supplier infrastructure to exert pressure.

But profit opportunities are mitigated by:

- the cost of funding growth; and

- new competitors entering the market relatively easily.

During the *maturity and decline phases*, profits tend to shift backwards in the value chain and end-use providers tend to struggle to stay profitable:

- supply infrastructure is well established and much of the products' value added is provided further back in the value chain;

- competitive pressure increases as growth slows; and

- development of distribution infrastructure creates new, larger customers with more bargaining power.

But these pressures are somewhat relieved because:

- there are usually only a few large competitors in the industry, so bargaining power can be concentrated; and

- it is very hard for new competitors to enter the market.

An example of the shift in bargaining power is provided by the PC industry. The early winners were pioneers such as IBM and Compaq. But today, the most profitable include the makers of hard disk technology, three or four companies back in the value chain, while the assemblers face razor-thin margins. Venerable IBM has all but abandoned PC manufacturing in favour of providing services to companies.[2]

Smart quotes

'In periods when product functionality is not yet good enough, in-tegrated companies that design and make end-use products typi-cally make the most money ... But when the large integrated players overshoot what their mainstream customers can use, the power to make money shifts away from activities where the standard, modular integration occurs. Competitive forces compel the suppliers to try to push the bleeding edge of performance. The power to capture at-tractive profits will shift in the value chain to these activities – activities that create steeper economies of scale and greater opportunities for differentiation.'

Clayton Christensen et al.,
'Skate to where the money will be', (HBR, Nov 2001)

How to cope with uncertainty

The only certainty with forecasting is that the forecasts will prove to be inaccurate. But usually they are close enough to the mark to add enough useful insight to make good strategic choices.

What uncertain events could sig-nificantly affect our profitability?

But sometimes there are just too many uncertainties. Will a new tech-nology take off or fail? Will government introduce a new piece of leg-islation affecting the industry? Will the market crash? These kinds of uncertainties cannot easily be forecast, yet they can have a significant effect on the outcome.

Smart quotes

'What we anticipate seldom occurs; what we least expected generally happens.'

Benjamin Disraeli

Scenario planning

When there is uncertainty, companies need to make decisions that will produce the best outcome on average and which avoid the worst-case outcomes.

The most common approach to developing strategy under uncertainty is scenario planning. Several different potential futures are forecast covering a range of likely combinations of events. By considering how each scenario will affect the company's performance, managers can find plans that are likely to be effective in a wide range of scenarios.

Sometimes, there are a relatively small number of uncertainties to consider – in this case, scenario planners can consider the full range of possible alternatives.

More often a few scenarios are chosen to fill in for a vast array of possible futures, giving managers a taste of the range of outcomes they could face, the kinds of challenges they will meet, and the risks they are subject to.

The construction industry is very dependent on the economic cycle. During recessions and slow-downs, the construction industry tends to get hit particularly hard. Therefore construction companies pay close attention to economic growth figures and government policy. In deciding whether to expand into new markets (a strategic commitment), a construction company will probably want to consider a range of scenarios:

● a long continuation of the construction boom;

● a period of relatively constant growth for five years followed by a typical business cycle;

- a short recession next year in which government acts aggressively by reducing interest rates and offering incentives for residential construction; and

- a long drawn out recession where demand for property construction is low.

By examining the potential risks and benefits inherent in each of these scenarios, the company can make the best decision.

Options

An alternative is to delay making important choices until after the critical uncertain events have taken place. That doesn't mean doing nothing. Some actions can usefully be taken now because they are likely to be valuable regardless of how things turn out. And some actions need to be taken now to give you the *option* to make choices later.

To give a more concrete example: your company is planning to build a copper mine on a known deposit, but it will only be worth building if the copper price rises 20%. If you don't buy the deposit now, then if the copper price rises, you'll lose out. But if you do buy it and build the mine and the copper price *doesn't* rise, the investment is wasted.

The best policy may be to buy the deposit, but delay building the mine until the copper price rises, giving you the option to do so later. In the worst case you have lost the small investment in the land, but not

Smart quotes

'Options provide flexibility. [A company with them] is more valuable than one without these options.'

Copeland et al., *Valuation*

> **Smart things to say**
>
> The greater the uncertainty, the greater the value of an option.

nearly as much as if you had built the mine. And in the best case, you have only slightly delayed the mine's development. So, buying the land now gives you the option to choose whether or not to the build the mine in the future.

> **Smart answers to tough questions**
>
> Q: What is an option worth?
>
> A: You can usually get a good estimate of the value of an option if you can make a fair guess[3] at:
>
> - The *probability* things will go well enough that you can exercise the option.
> - The *benefit* you expect to receive if things go well enough that you exercise the option.
> - The *cost* you expect to avoid by <u>not</u> exercising the option if things go badly.
>
> ### No option to delay decision
> Investment decision must be made before uncertainties are resolved
>
> ### Option to delay decision
> Incur a small cost to retain the option to invest later if uncertain event is favourable
>
> **Fig. 11.3** Estimating the value of an option.

How to approach extreme uncertainty

When uncertainty is very high, such as when entering emerging industries, planning becomes all but impossible and even options become hard to value. The best hope for success is 'guided opportunism'.

- Find an industry where customer value appears to indicate a highly profitable business opportunity, but enormous uncertainty.

- Generate as many opportunities as possible:

  - try plausible products and business models; and
  - purchase cheap, broad options against some of the bigger uncertainties.

- Stay flexible and adapt to circumstances as they arise.

- When opportunities for business success present themselves, pounce on them.

Just getting started is a major step towards generating opportunities.

Small businesses often don't end up in the business they started in. Instead, faced with uncertainty, many entrepreneurs determined to make money and willing to be opportunistic will eventually find a good idea.

Smart quotes

'A tree that is unbending is easily broken ... The flexible will overcome.'

Lao Tsu, *Tao Te Ching*

One small enterprise in Hong Kong started out in telecommunications consulting, shifted into developing-country market research, switched to providing a service to help foreign investors find joint-venture partners and finally found a successful formula in investor relations.

The battle for dominance amongst Internet retailers seemed to be inspired in a large part by this kind of thinking. It was clear that getting and locking-in customers represented the best way to generate lots of opportunities for profit, even if it was not at all clear how money would ever be made. So the initial battle was one for customers. Only once a customer base was established did companies start to look hard for ways to make money from their customers. Unfortunately, customers turned out to be a lot harder to lock-in than expected. Those companies, like Amazon, that managed it are now finding out whether they can make a decent profit from their customer base.

Guided opportunism is not an excuse to avoid planning. It is a risky strategy, so if your competitors are able to plan ahead, they will have an advantage. If they are as in the dark as you are, then go for it.

Summary of main points

- Understanding market dynamics allows a company to predict where profits can be made and make better decisions:

  - product lifecycles have a big impact on profit opportunities, even changing which parts of the value chain are most attractive; and
  - other long-term trends also need to be taken into account when looking for market opportunities.

- In many cases uncertainty makes market dynamics difficult to forecast. In this situation, companies can find ways to buy 'options' that let them delay major commitments until the uncertainty is resolved.

Notes

1   After World War II, there were an unusually large number of babies born in many countries, creating a demographic bulge.

2   Dell is a notable exception to this rule, largely because it has taken a different approach to competition. For more on Dell's competitive approach see 'Focus on what you do best' in Chapter 12, 'Creating a Lasting Competitive Advantage'.

3   A full treatment of options is far beyond the scope of this book.

12 Creating a Lasting Competitive Advantage

How the competitive battle is fought

Market dynamics (see Chapter 11, 'Forecasting Market Dynamics') was all about finding good market opportunities. But however attractive the market, if companies hope for decent profits, then they must be prepared to stand up and fight their competitors for them. And even if a company finds itself in a relatively unattractive market, competitive dominance may yet allow the company to have a successful business.

Using efficient customer value creation as a competitive weapon

The most obvious and often best approach to competition is simply to be better at providing efficient customer value creation than competitors. If your products are more highly valued, or your prices can be kept lower, you are bound to do better than your competitors.

To create a sustainable competitive advantage in delivering efficient customer value creation, you need to be able to perform some fundamental part of the business significantly better than your competitors.

Smart quotes

'Strategic competition can be thought of as the process of wooing customers.'

Michael Porter

This means developing a core competence in one or more of the following critical business processes:

- better understanding of customer needs and ability to respond quickly with effective solutions to these needs;

- use of technological expertise in new product development;

- technological innovation resulting in new products or improved production efficiency;

- faster learning and better knowledge-sharing to make technologies more efficient; and

- more efficient management: a higher proportion of time spent on value-creating tasks and more effective processes for decision-making and resource allocation.

Companies looking for quick fixes to propel themselves ahead are unlikely to be able to maintain a long-term advantage over companies that are systematically better at improving their key business processes. Therefore, excellent management of these core processes is the key to long-term success.

Focus on what you do best

A narrow focus can help to provide competitive advantage in these processes. Focus on one customer group to meet its needs better. Focus on a few technologies to make them core competencies. Focus on a single goal to focus decision-making and improve effective use of resources and management time. By focusing, you can create a competitor-beating advantage.

When selecting a strategy, it is advisable to take a different approach to your competitors.

- Competing directly with the same strategy tends to produce a winner-takes-all outcome, or a mutually destructive arms race. By selecting different strategic approaches, it is more likely that you will create a sustainable competitive advantage over some part of the market.

- You have more chance to play to your strengths. In contrast, you are likely to find it hard to copy a strategy that another company uses successfully. Unless you are better at *something* than your competitors, you cannot expect to win.

- Competition becomes a battle of different market philosophies – there is far more opportunity for creativity, improvement and finesse than in a head-to-head battle which tends to become focused on a small range of issues.

For example, Dell has taken a radically different approach to its competitors. Dell has chosen to focus on direct orders and build-to-order manufacturing that provides lower inventory costs and greater customization, while competitors focus on more efficient build-to-stock, and distribute through the safer retail channel, which can provide better customer service.

Smart quotes

'From a competitive standpoint, the problem with operational effectiveness is that best practices are easily emulated ... Such competition produces absolute improvements, but relative improvements for no one. Strategic positioning attempts to achieve sustainable competitive advantage by preserving what is distinctive about a company. It means performing different activities, or performing similar activities in different ways.'

Michael Porter

Not all industries give competitors the option to select radically different strategies. On the whole, industries where there are few available strategic alternatives are more competitive and less profitable. If you find yourself in a head-to-head battle, the rule is: make your competitor respond to your initiatives – make sure your company is the one that comes up with the new ideas. If your competitors are just trying to keep up, they will find it much harder to get ahead.

Smart quotes

'The good fighter ... takes the initiative and influences the reaction of his opponent.'

Bruce Lee, Martial Artist

Resource dominance – the heavy artillery of competitive advantage

But efficient customer value creation is by no means the only path to competitive success, nor indeed the easiest.

A simpler approach is to prevent other companies from ever getting the chance to compete with you. Then, it doesn't take genius to make money. The trick to this approach is to dominate the industry's limited resources.

Almost every industry has resources that companies need in order to compete. You can't compete in gold production if you don't have access to a low-cost gold mine, and there aren't a whole heap of them to go around. Companies that own them have a licence to print money.

What are the limited strategic resources in our industry? Who controls them?

Another example can be seen in the soft-drink industry, where fast-food chain distribution is in effect a limited resource. Controlling this resource gives a provider a large and untouchable share of the total soft-drink market. When PepsiCo struck a deal with McDonalds in the US, it won a big share of the US soft-drink market. The increase in market share had nothing to do with customer choice – they still went into McDonalds' restaurants asking for Coke, but they got Pepsi. And PepsiCo didn't stop there – they also bought fast-food chains such as Pizza Hut and KFC, partly to dominate these important distribution channels.

More recently Coca-Cola faced intense scrutiny from competition authorities about its attempt to control another key limited distribution resource – the soft-drink fridges in small stores.

The recent auctions for 3G licences in Europe show how valuable limited resources can be. On average bidders paid US$500 per capita for licences in the UK and Germany – a total of around $46 billion in Germany alone. Without a licence, companies cannot compete in the next generation of mobile telephony, so companies are prepared to pay most of the value of future profits to secure them. In essence, the auctions have enabled governments to appropriate much of the value available in the industry before it has even begun. The companies that own licences must hope that the 3G mobile business turns out to be more lucrative than most people are forecasting – if their hopes are realized then, as holders of the critical industry resources, they will gain all the benefits.

In contrast, licences were given away for free in Japan – the government essentially handed billions of dollars to the chosen companies.

Most industries have limited resources somewhere in their value chain. And competitors that can control these resources will have an unbeatable advantage. In these industries, the battle for competitive advantage comes down to a battle over these limited resources. Governments that are keen to maintain high levels of competition try to ensure that these resources are made freely available to competitors. For companies, the aim is to get control of these resources cheaply.

The economics of monopoly

When one competitor controls all of a limited resource in an industry it can get a monopoly – no one else can compete. Most often this limited resource is government approval. And some of the most notorious and long-lived monopolies have been government run or sanctioned.

Monopolies are generally bad for customers since, freed from competition, monopolists have all the bargaining power over customers. They can generally raise prices to increase their margins – so long as they don't lose too many customers in the process they'll be better off.

But even worse than transferring value from customers to suppliers, monopolies also reduce the total value of an industry.

The first reason is that when prices are higher there are fewer customers. Since the total value of an industry is the total value of all the customers' satisfied needs, the industry is actually producing less value in total for the industry participants to share.

The second reason is that monopolists tend to be inefficient. Without any competitive incentive for efficiency and improvement, monopolists waste valuable economic resources – especially employees' time. If these resources could be freed up, they could be used elsewhere in the economy to produce value.

So, not surprisingly, most capitalist governments try to prevent monopolies from forming.[1]

Monopoly may be a path to easy wealth, but it has its risks. Inefficiency and customer resentment are a pent-up force. When the monopoly is eventually broken, customers will flee. When British Telecom's monopoly ended, customers left in droves and only began to return after a major restructuring and improvements in customer service. (Even governments cannot keep feeding the cash-sucking beasts that they've created forever, although many have shown an astounding tolerance.)

Niche monopolies

Niche focus strategies generally aim to give a company monopoly over a small market segment. By focusing specifically on one segment it is easier to gain a competitive advantage. Other competitors seeking to win the niche will also have to target it specifically or have a very compelling whole-market offering.

Sometimes the small size of a niche can actually provide a barrier to other entrants. If the efficient scale of production is similar to the size of the niche, a potential competitor would need to believe they could win over the whole market if they wished to enter and still make money.

While niches provide a form of monopoly, they tend to be relatively weak. Customers often have the benefit of good substitute products – those aimed at the wider market.

Using networking effects to create a competitive advantage

Networking effects are a special class of limited resource in which the winner takes all.

There is a rule that the value of a telephone network increases much faster than the number of people connected to it. Clearly it is far less useful to own a telephone if there is only one other person to call (especially if you don't get on with them!). As the network increases in size, there are more people for each person to connect with.

Smart quotes

'The value of a network increases with the square of the number of people connected to it.'

Metcalf's Law

When two networks compete against each other, then as soon as one network gets a little larger, it becomes substantially more valuable to customers. More people join the larger, more valuable network, increasing its advantage over its smaller competitor. Eventually, there is just one winner.

A similar situation affected the market for video cassette recorders. Sony's Betamax was the earlier entrant and was considered to be slightly technically superior, yet JVC's VHS format managed to obtain a market lead fairly early on. Today the VHS standard is the only one that survives.

It is slightly surprising that the market for VCRs can be considered as a 'network', but it shares many features with other types of network. The value of a given format of video cassette increases with the number of people who use it – more movies are released in that format, video stores keep more copies of movies in that format and there are more people to swap cassettes with. So as soon as the VHS format got a market lead, there was a lot of pressure on people to use that format. It became the de facto standard for the whole industry.

Network effects provide us with the final piece in the dot.com puzzle. In many markets it was believed that there were strong network effects. The larger sites would be able to offer more services, making them more popular. So, the theory ran, get big quickly and you can control the market standard. Once you dominated the market, you would become impregnable to competition.

The auction site, eBay, is one networking effect success story. The more people who use it, the more buyers there are for each product making the auction process more reliable and attracting more sellers. The more sellers there are, the greater the variety of products on offer, attracting more buyers.

For governments looking to protect customers from monopoly power, network effects present a difficult dilemma. Often the efficiency of a single large network really is much greater than several smaller ones. In making telecommunications a competitive market, many countries have seen that, even with government protection, smaller competitors cannot easily compete on equal terms. The best approach is a compromise – the network is maintained as a regulated monopoly, while customer sales and service is made a competitive industry.

How to change the rules of the game to favour your organization

If the mountain won't come to Mohammed ...

If you can't win with what you have, change the rules of the game. If you don't happen to have access to the limited resources in the industry, change the situation so that they are less important. Change the standards to favour you. Make your competitive advantages the most important ones.

Smart quotes

'The people who get on in this world are the people who get up and look for the circumstances they want, and if they can't find them, make them.'

George Bernard Shaw

For example, if you are making DVD players and you can't get a licence to incorporate the industry-leading sound standard in your DVD players, does this mean you are sunk? Not if you can convince customers that another sound standard is in fact better. Or convince them that sound quality is less important than picture quality, where perhaps you have the advantage.

And there is always government – the most swayable of rule changers. Lobbying for market conditions that favour your own company is a trick many companies have learned. In some developing countries, the ability to sway governments is so important that it represents the most powerful competitive advantage a company can possess.

The benefits of cooperation

There is one final topic to deal with in competitive advantage. That is cooperation.

Colluding with the enemy

One way to use cooperation to your advantage is to collude directly with your competitors so that you can share the benefits of monopoly power.

If you can't beat them, join them.

The best known examples of collusion are the supplier cartels, De Beers (in diamonds) and OPEC (in oil). In both cases, the aim is to hold prices at above competitive market rates by restricting supply, and sharing the benefits between the cartel's members. (See box for how restricting supply can raise prices.) In oligopolies (i.e. where a few companies control the market) the alternative is often destructive competition.[2]

For many countries this kind of collusive price-fixing is illegal, for obvious reasons. But there are ways to collude without having to explicitly discuss quotas and pricing. So long as there are only a few competitors

Smart people to have on your side: Adam Smith

How limiting supply can increase prices
'The market price of every particular commodity is regulated by the proportion between the quantity which is actually brought to market, and the demand of those who are willing to pay the price ... which must be paid in order to bring it thither.

'When the quantity of any commodity which is brought to market falls short of the effectual demand, all those who are willing to pay ... cannot be supplied with the quantity which they want ... some of them will be willing to give more. A competition will immediately begin among them, and the market price will rise ... Hence the exorbitant price of the necessities of life during the blockade of a town or in a famine.'

and each competitor's actions on prices and volumes are visible to the others, it is relatively easy to collude tacitly.

Take, for example, guarantees to match a competitor's price. These customer-friendly guarantees hide a sinister intent. By removing any advantage for price-cutting, they act as a way for competitors to tacitly collude to maintain higher prices!

But fortunately, many cartels fail. Often prices and volumes are very hard for competitors to discern. In many industries, for example, 'list price' is rarely paid by customers, most of whom receive large discounts. Therefore, there is no way to tell whether a competitor is cheating and no easy way to discipline the cheaters.

Even a small amount of external competition can threaten a cartel – a small company can gain share very rapidly at the expense of a cartel and prevent it maintaining prices.

Smart quotes

'Successful Japanese competitors have constructed webs of alliances to acquire competencies at low cost.'

Gary Hamel and C.K. Prahalad,
'The Core Competence of the Corporation' (*HBR* May–June 1990)

Smart quotes

'A well-developed ability to create and sustain fruitful collaborations gives companies a significant competitive leg up … Temporary disadvantages from giving something to an ally can create long-run advantages.'

Rosabeth Moss Kanter

Using partnerships to build your competitive resources

Close relationships with suppliers often offer the opportunity for efficiency gains through knowledge sharing and organizational efficiencies.

Companies benefit from partnerships and alliances by:

- using the other company's core competencies and limited resources; and

- managing processes together with suppliers to cut costs, capital requirements, inventories, ordering delays etc.

Relationships between companies are becoming more common as more companies discover the potential benefits. For example, companies are increasingly building 'strategic alliances' with their suppliers.

In Chapter 11, 'Forecasting Market Dynamics', we spoke about supplier relationships in combative terms of 'bargaining power'. But partnerships may be able to provide sufficient value that both parties are better off in the long-run.

Value-nurturing industries

When companies share an industry for a long time, it is worthwhile for the industry participants to cooperate to increase the value of the whole industry so that everyone can benefit. In some industries, customers, competitors and suppliers work together to set standards and develop industry infrastructure.

Competition in value-nurturing industries is kept to 'productive' competition – improvements in efficient customer value creation rather than the use of bargaining power or attempts to eliminate competition. Often competitors divide the market into segments and avoid head-to-head 'destructive' competition.

Some competitors find that they meet the same companies in different capacities, sometimes as suppliers, sometimes as customers and sometimes as competitors. In this case it is hardly worth fighting to eliminate a competitor from one industry since competitors can retaliate in another. Instead there are strong incentives to maintain healthy relations.

Centres of excellence

Some locations seem particularly good places to be for certain industries. Sometimes there are good reasons – Johannesburg is a centre of excellence for gold mining, because there are many gold deposits there. But how can you explain why Silicon Valley is a centre of IT excellence? Or why Italy is a centre of excellence for leather and shoes? The reasons are largely historical, but once a location gains an advantage it is self-reinforcing because companies in these centres of excellence are more competitive than those based elsewhere (see box).

Smart people to have on your side: Michael Porter

Industry clusters
Michael Porter has a framework that explains why these centres of excellence, or 'industry clusters' are so enduring – they provide companies who operate there with significant operational advantages in four ways:

- *Resources*. Clusters usually develop where there is an abundance of key industry resources.
- *Networks*. Clusters often develop where there are already rich networks of related companies and suitable infrastructure and skills. In turn infrastructure and related industries form around the cluster.
- *Competition*. The nature of competition is important to the formation of clusters. Where the competition is value-nurturing and based on customer value, companies in the cluster improve their efficiency rapidly. The presence of competitors also allows new ideas to flow quickly around the cluster.
- *Customers*. Clusters often form around large customer markets or pockets of very demanding customers. Once formed, the cluster can attract the biggest and most discerning customers. Customers provide feedback and a large-scale local market for producers.

Michael Porter was most interested in how governments can help to nurture these clusters and provide conditions favourable to their formation. For companies, there is a lesson too: be close to the competition.

Smart answers to tough questions

Q: How do you win a competitive battle?

A:

- *Focus* on one broad goal at a time and put all available resources into achieving it – don't get distracted by small gains that sap resources. Know the costs and benefits and aim for the most valuable goals first. Fight to monopolize the critical limited resources early.
- *Differentiate and play to your strengths* – differentiate your goals and strengths from your competitors rather than try to compete on equal terms. Force your competitors to compete where you are strongest and they are weakest.
- *Synergize* – get the most from all your resources: look for synergies; make your resources and strengths complement each other; use other people's resources to bolster your own; look for network effects; use your strengths in as many contexts as possible.
- *Improve constantly* – always look to improve your strengths and resources. Put your effort into developing skills where the pay-off is biggest – initially, weaknesses can often be fixed relatively easily, but later it usually pays to focus on building your strengths rather than weaknesses.
- *Retain tactical flexibility* – where possible create options and maintain flexibility (but don't pursue flexibility if it compromises focus). Set broad plans of actions rather than planning detailed tactics in advance – tactics are best decided on the spot in accordance with the needs of the situation.
- *Know more than your competitors and surprise them* – understand the situation better. Know your competitors' strengths and intentions so they cannot surprise you. Force your competitors to respond to you. Use the initiative to manoeuvre them into a position where you can surprise them with a fast, powerful assault.

Summary of main points

- Competitive advantage can rest in being better at efficient customer value creation – to be sustainable, it usually requires a core competence in a key process such as innovation or resource allocation.

- A more effective approach is to avoid competition by dominating a limited resource in the industry.

- In many industries it is possible to use standards or network effects to create a strong competitive advantage.

- It is also possible to use alliances and resources as a way to acquire core competencies, limited resources and efficiencies.

- Industries that promote value-creating competition tend to be better for all industry participants.

Notes

1   Central planning advocates have tended to support monopolies on the grounds that competition requires duplication of skills and resources. But history has shown that the benefits of competitive pressure on efficiency and innovation outweigh the additional costs unless there are significant network effects (see section on Using networking effects to create a competitive advantage, p. 168).

2   In some markets, game theory predicts that competitors should be willing to drive each other to destruction. In many building products markets, for example, competitors appear willing to price-cut the entire industry out of business.

13 A Systematic Approach to Planning

What are you planning for?

Planning is a very important component of management. Good planning ensures that:

- managers consider long-term strategic commitments inherent in their actions;

- managers can intervene early when strategic conflicts arise;

- resources are deployed where they can produce the most profit; and

- actions are coordinated between different parts of the company.

Given the importance of planning, companies are understandably keen to make it a formal company-wide process.

Typically, planning in companies falls into three types:

- *major ad hoc decisions* (e.g. new products, strategic commitments, alliances and major expenditures);

- *regular strategic reviews*; and

- *regular reviews of financial performance and cash needs.*

Planning ad hoc capital investments

Any large expenditure represents both a long-term strategic commitment and a financial investment and should therefore be made carefully. New projects require a detailed strategic and financial justification.

An added advantage of a detailed proposal is that once the project is under way, the proposal's expectations can be compared to actual outcomes. This provides a useful tool for managing the project and feedback on how well managers were able to plan.

The capital expenditure allocation process is one of the most important levers available to senior managers to coordinate activities in the company and guide strategy.

Smart answers to tough questions

Q: When reviewing a proposal for expenditure, senior managers should consider the following questions:

A:
- Can the expenditure be expected to produce an adequate long-term return on investors' capital?
- How much risk is associated with the project?
  - What are the market uncertainties?
  - What competitor actions could threaten the project?
- Does the project fit with the existing strategy of the company, and with other projects being run in the company?
- What new strategic commitments does the investment require?

A sample investment proposal

The basic idea
To upgrade the brick factory in Springfield to benefit from state-of-the-art developments in technology.

The likely returns
The initial cost will be $10,000,000. The return will be provided by sales of surplus land and obsolete equipment – $2,000,000 – and a lower operating cost of $0.20 per unit produced. Maintenance and replacement costs are also expected to be lower. A rate of return on investment of 17% is anticipated.

(Detailed analysis of return economics attached.)

Market risks/opportunities
The technology is well developed, but will be new to our team, so we must learn how to use it quickly. There is always a risk of radical new technological development, but history has shown that new ideas take several years to develop and we are not aware of any major new ideas on the horizon.

(Detailed market forecasts and risk assessment attached.)

Competitive risks/opportunities
Our major competitor is using a technology similar to the plant's current operations, but has newer equipment. Given this, it is unlikely it would make economic sense for them to reinvest further capital in new technology in the near future. The competitor will not have the option of a price war since we will have lower operating costs. The new technology is also likely to improve product quality. And new inventory and production management systems will allow faster order response times for most customers, particularly in the architectural segment.

(Detailed competitor analysis attached.)

Fit with corporate strategy
The key corporate strategic goal is to be the preferred supplier for large

projects in a small number of the highest profit market segments. This goal should be aided by this technology (see competitive opportunities).

Capabilities assessment
The project will involve new technologies and management skills that may also prove useful elsewhere in the company. In particular, the new plant will make use of 'quality circles' and could be used as a model for the whole company.

None of the technologies is expected to present serious implementation difficulties, but plans include additional time and cost for training to take account of any contingencies that arise.

Strategic fit with other projects
Capabilities and technologies developed on this project could be used to improve quality and cost in other business areas. We already have other operations based in Springfield and co-location could help to reduce costs.

Annual planning and budgeting

While ad hoc project assessment is valuable, most companies find it useful to engage in an annual planning and budgeting process. The benefits are that it:

- provides an assessment of likely funding needs for each division;

- helps to identify brands, products, markets, divisions etc., in need of additional management attention;

- allows senior managers to audit divisions' strategic initiatives and coordinate them with initiatives elsewhere in the company;

- allows senior managers to identify opportunities emerging in the company that may become a focus for the company in the future; and

- highlights major issues for long-term performance, so that appropriate action can be taken in advance.

Killer questions

Does the company have a coherent plan that takes account of the needs of all its businesses and provides the basis for coordinating their strategic objectives?

While annual planning is a very useful exercise, it can cause a lot of friction in the company:

- divisional managers resent the burden on their time; and

- managers fear having their budgets reduced and fear being held accountable for meeting forecasts subject to uncertainty.

Does our planning and budgeting process reward the right behaviours?

Managers are often tempted to provide inaccurate information in an effort to win themselves greater rewards, greater influence and more project capital. Inevitably, this only damages the company and leads to more conflict. Senior managers must be very careful to avoid creating perverse incentives.

Budgeting and strategic planning are separate processes (allocating funds versus setting direction), but most companies combine them to reduce the burden on busy managers. The combination may not al-

Smart quotes

'Traditional budgeting processes waste time, distort decisions and turn honest managers into schemers.'

Michael Jensen, 'Corporate Budgeting is Broken –
Let's Fix It' (*HBR* Nov 2001)

ways serve the best interests of either process: strategy being creative, contemplative and long-term; budgeting being analytical, commercial and shorter-term.

A sample annual plan/budget

Market dynamics – opportunities and threats
The brick industry is likely to see falling revenues over the next ten years as new, cheaper materials become more popular. A shortage of brick-layers is likely to increase costs for customers and speed industry decline, although we are investing in trade schools to help train more.

One potential growth area is high-end architectural projects, where our materials are featured in overseas designs currently in fashion. There may also be opportunities in civil projects, which should experience a short-term surge in the wake of government spending increases on schools and hospitals.

Competitive advantage – strengths/weaknesses/critical resources
We have a strong advantage in the high-margin architectural sector where we have close relationships with key decision-makers on many major projects. Our materials are also better suited for these applications. Our investment in trade schools means that many bricklayers are most familiar with our products.

We have a weak position in the civil sector, where our competitors have more influential local government contacts. In theory this shouldn't affect tender decisions, but in reality it makes it harder for us to meet tender requirements prepared with other competitors' products in mind.

Major initiatives for the coming year
- Continue to develop the trade schools;
- market overseas designs to the architectural market;
- develop new products for the architectural segment to suit new designs;
- create a specialist team to prepare government tenders; and
- look at the economics of plant upgrades/rationalization.

Expected performance for the year
Performance is expected to be slightly stronger this year – overall revenues will be lower, but growth in the high-profit architectural sector should compensate. Our initial budget is similar to last year.

(See attached monthly financial projections.)

Long-term strategic plan
The main issue is the declining market. The strategic approach will be to focus on the more attractive areas of the market where we enjoy a competitive advantage. The remaining market will be served where it remains profitable to do so. Capacity will be reduced through plant closures, and selective plant upgrades will be made to keep costs competitive in our key segments.

Five-year strategic goals
- Capture 80% of the architectural sector and promote growth in this market;
- win 50% of major civil tenders at 5% margin;
- double the number of bricklayers graduating annually through the company's training schools; and
- lower per-unit operating costs by 5% from technology upgrades/ plant rationalization.

Expected five-year performance
Long-tem performance will suffer from the industry decline, especially as there is little prospect for industry-wide capacity reduction. But the next three years look to be strong for the industry and particularly for the company.

(See attached five-year financial projections and historical review.)

Major financial risks/opportunities
The main issue is whether the envisaged revival in the architectural sector actually eventuates. The Springfield plant upgrade should help to increase market share in the architectural segment, but there is also a risk that it will take longer to get operational than anticipated.

(See attached analysis of financial risks.)

Annual planning and budgeting: investor communications

Planning has another role – investor communications. For an investor, the value of a company depends not just on current performance, but on the long-term stream of returns they can expect to receive. The planning process allows directors to keep an eye on the long-term prospects for shareholders.

Smart answers to tough questions

Q: How are stakeholders' interests protected?

A: Corporate governance.

Corporate governance refers to the system for ensuring that companies protect the interests of the company's stakeholders. In the US system of corporate governance, the managers have a responsibility to protect the interests of shareholders *only*. This might seem rather unfair – what about the interests of employees, lenders and the wider community? The rationale is that these other interests are already well protected by the law and by market forces – the primary problem of corporate governance is the conflict of interest between shareholders and managers. (This approach is not universal – in Germany, for example, managers also have a responsibility to workers.)

Corporate governance is applied through a board of directors chosen by the shareholders. The board has the power to hire and fire senior managers, hold them responsible for their performance and participate in major investment and strategy decisions. The aim is to ensure that managers act to provide the greatest possible returns for shareholders.

There is a great deal of debate as to whether boards of directors are sufficiently powerful to protect shareholders' interests. For example, CEO salaries have risen rapidly – the CEOs of many large companies earn tens of millions of dollars even when their companies are not performing well. Is it a sign of poor corporate governance, or simply a reflection of the great value of CEO talent?

Do our share-holders have confidence in our plans?

The planning process enables managers to compare their own expectations with those of the shareholders. If there is a big disparity between internal valuations and the share price, perhaps investors don't know about all the initiatives that the company is planning? Or perhaps they do, but are just far more sceptical of them!

Why does it matter? Because the ultimate test of a company's success is the returns it can provide to shareholders. Senior managers will be judged by the share price. And the company's ability to raise capital for new projects depends greatly on the market's assessment of its future performance.

CEOs of public companies always keep one eye on their share price!

Can strategy be planned?

The formal planning and budgeting procedure described above enables top managers to influence important decisions within their companies.

However, some management thinkers argue that successful strategy cannot emerge from formal planning alone. New ideas usually spring up from all sorts of unexpected corners. Companies struggle, experiment and post-rationalize in response to market forces until they eventually hit on a successful formula. Operational managers are always looking for new ways to offer more to customers so, over time, the company's activities expand.

Rather, planning serves a different role – to focus resources on a more limited number of activities: those that work well together require the same long-term commitments and have the most promising futures.

Smart people to have on your side: Henry Mintzberg

Crafting strategy
Mintzberg is a strong critic of formal planning as a method for setting strategy. He believes that formal planning has an important role to play in: 'strategic programming – the articulation and elaboration of strategies that already exist'. However, he does not believe that strategic planning can be relied on to develop strategy because it is neither a sufficiently creative process, nor in harmony with the way managers actually develop strategy in practice:

- Top-level managers and planners do not have access to sufficient information. They lack the operational knowledge of their workers, and miss many small but important pieces of information on emerging trends.
- The formal planning process is too slow. Lacking sufficient information, companies need to be experimental to develop strategy; but annual planning cycles give little opportunity for dynamic development of strategy. Furthermore, the idea that conditions will remain unchanged until the next planning round is far fetched.
- Formal planning tends to produce unimaginative strategies that try to do everything at once. There is little incentive to take risks: planning provides an over-formalized approach to an essentially creative activity; and it fails to take full account of resource limitations.

As an example he describes how the Film Board of Canada's highly commended and successful strategy emerged. FBC never planned to get into commissioning and distributing feature-length movies. In fact they actively chose to avoid it. One customer however came to them with an overly long movie and, in looking to help this customer, FBC developed distribution skills and theatre contacts. The project was successful and they were soon able to offer a similar service to other filmmakers. The service was so popular that FBC's strategy was altered to explicitly focus on this activity.

To Mintzberg this illustrates that strategy is not something that is carefully planned, but something that emerges from being active and responsive in an industry.

So strategy creation should be the result of a dynamic interaction between operations (finding new ideas), and planning (deciding which to pursue and which to drop). (See box.)

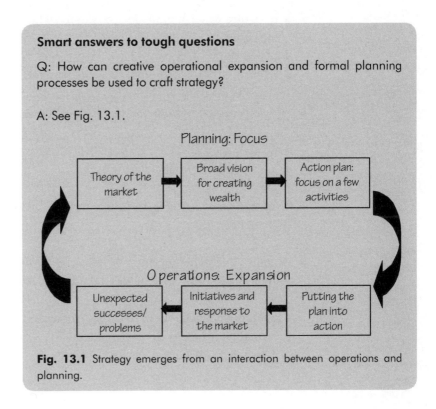

Smart answers to tough questions

Q: How can creative operational expansion and formal planning processes be used to craft strategy?

A: See Fig. 13.1.

Planning: Focus

Theory of the market → Broad vision for creating wealth → Action plan: focus on a few activities

Operations: Expansion

Unexpected successes/ problems ← Initiatives and response to the market ← Putting the plan into action

Fig. 13.1 Strategy emerges from an interaction between operations and planning.

If the process is to be successful, employees should be encouraged to take the initiative in trying new ideas, meeting new customer needs and experimenting with new strategic approaches. Empowerment therefore helps strategy formation.

Summary of main points

- Companies use formal planning processes:

  - to ensure strategic issues are considered when undertaking major initiatives;
  - to coordinate actions; and
  - to ensure that managers look to the long term.

- Typically, companies use two planning processes:

  - an ad hoc process for new project proposals; and
  - a systematic annual planning cycle.

- Long-term planning is essential if managers are to deliver long-term value to investors.

- Strategy development cannot be left to the formal planning process alone. Instead, strategy emerges dynamically from:

  - operations, which tends to expand activities; and
  - formal planning by senior management, who aim to eliminate activities to improve resource efficiency.

14 Designing an Effective Organization

How much organization does your company need?

Any large task requires coordination between people. The more complex the task, the tougher the challenge. The bigger and more complex a business becomes, the greater the need for a formal organizational structure to aid coordination.

To illustrate, let's look at the difference between how a company of 10 people and one of 200 deal with an organizational challenge:

Large company	Small company
'Is that Business Development? Can I speak to Sanjay Gupta?' 'Sanjay here.' 'Hey Sanjay! It's Peter Ilic from Sales, we're totally bogged down here preparing tenders, can you get a team together to help us out?' 'I'll see whether I can free some people up, but I've got to tell you, we're pretty busy. We'll need to scrounge people from Marketing. I'd better talk to HR. Can you send me a memo on what you need?' 'I'll speak to the sales team and send you something tomorrow. Can we meet on Thursday to discuss it?' 'I'll check if I'm free. I'll also invite Bronwyn Jacobs from HR along if that's OK?' 'Fine. Look, I'll see you then.'	Nikki: 'Hey, Lin, can you help me deal with a couple of tenders?' Lin: 'Sure Nikki. I'm pretty busy though. Mike, can you give us a hand?' Mike: 'Yeah, no problem guys.'

Whatever you do, a large complex company is going to be far tougher to organize than a small one. (But even if your interest lies just in small companies, there's a lot to learn from this chapter.)

Organizational structure can greatly aid cooperation and efficiency by:

- providing clear duties so everyone can work out who is responsible for performing each activity;

- ensuring people who need to cooperate have access to each other; and

- grouping together people who need to share information, knowledge or resources, or require a similar culture.

Designing an organization is not easy and there are difficult trade-offs. Should you group people by product or market, for example? And because many tasks involve a great deal of coordination, it's hard to work out which people to group together and which to separate – if you're not careful you can end up erecting barriers to efficiency.

Here we present the ideas behind organizational design. Hopefully these ideas will help you understand which organizational features are improving performance and which are hindering it.

Smart quotes

'Organizational structures rarely result from systematic, methodical planning. Rather they evolve over time, in fits and starts, shaped more by politics than by policies. The haphazard nature of the resulting structures is a source of constant frustration to senior executives'

Michael Goold and Andrew Campbell,
'Do You Have a Well-Designed Organization?' (HBR, March 2002)

Smart people to have on your side: Henry Mintzberg

Five generic organizational forms
According to Mintzberg, there are five distinct organizational structures. Each organization should select the one that best meets its particular needs. (See table below.)

Structure	Appropriate for	Key features
Simple structure	Entrepreneurial ventures or organizations undergoing radical transformation	Single autocratic leader directly supervizing a somewhat informal organization.
Professional bureaucracy	Professional services firms – independent experts with standardized skills	Large network of trainers and analysts support independent same-skill operations. Emphasis on training and corporate culture to maintain standards.
Machine bureaucracy	Large-scale organization of a simple process	Highly standardized and carefully controlled procedures. Large management structure supervizing activities.
Divisionalized form	Managing several units in a very large company.	Performance controlled at the top level. Business units can take many forms.
Adhocracy	Highly innovative/dynamic companies.	High level of inter-team liaison. Fluid organization. Big support network to help small teams to access key resources.

Design approach: focus on critical processes

All organizations perform a function – a company is a system for turning equipment, materials and employee time into products and services. For example, an airline is a system for getting people from one place to another.

To achieve this, the company must perform a series of smaller processes, each contributing towards the function of the organization as a whole. For an airline, these processes are:

- schedule the aircraft and crew ready for each flight;

- sell tickets to passengers;

- get passengers and baggage on and off the flights at airports;

- keep customers happy while in-flight; and

- ensure the aircraft are safely maintained.

In turn, each process can be divided into individual tasks that can be performed by small teams. For example, as part of getting passengers on and off flights, a team of check-in assistants is assembled at Paris Charles de Gaulle airport to check tickets and collect passengers' luggage for the flights.

Once the organization is divided into processes, the organization structure can be built around them.

Processes that can benefit from coordination should be grouped together to make communication easier; similarly, those servicing the same customers. Processes that can benefit from sharing resources or knowledge should be performed in the same location to make sharing easier; similarly, those with similar technologies or people with similar specializations. Businesses with similar cultures should go together and be separated from those with very different cultures.

But often there are conflicts between these ideals. If you have to choose between an organization focused on its products or one focused on its geographical markets, which should you choose?

> **Killer questions**
>
> What processes are critical to our competitive advantage? Does our organizational structure reflect this?

The answer is not always easy. But the key is identifying which processes and links between processes are the most important and dealing with their needs first. Other processes can be fitted around them in the organizational structure as efficiently as possible.

Priority must go to those processes that are critical to the company's competitive advantage. For example, if a competitive advantage centres on a technology, then priority goes to grouping together processes related to this technology. On the other hand, if providing customer service is critical, then priority goes to processes that serve the different customer groups.

Organizational simplicity through modular design

In addition, you might want to aim for simplicity. If an organization becomes too complex, it is hard to figure out who is responsible for what. If problems occur, it is hard to identify where the problem lies. In complex organizations, changing one part of the organization might mean altering most of the structure because processes are so entangled.

Modular design provides an approach to simplifying organizations. It is an approach borrowed from engineering in which strict rules are applied with the aim of making the resulting organization very much simpler, without losing too much efficiency (see box on next page).

The benefits and problems of hierarchy

Process design, and especially modular design, tends to lead to very hierarchical organizations. There are real benefits to this. Foremost is

> ### Smart answers to tough questions
>
> Q: How do you make an organization simpler?
>
> A: Use modular design:
> - each unit has a single, clear, easily-communicated role;
> - each unit contains a great deal of interaction within it, but as little interaction as possible with the rest of the organization;
> - each unit is divided into a small number (3–7) of sub-units – few enough to keep track of with our limited human minds;
> - units should be ordered into a strict hierarchy with each sub-unit interacting only with other sub-units of the same 'parent';
> - units should as far as possible operate in linear order, interacting only with immediately preceding and following units;
> - interactions between units should be simple, limited and rarely changed; and
> - units that perform the same function should be identical so that design complexity is reduced and more opportunities for sharing resources are possible.

that top-level management can use the hierarchy to control the entire organization. When coordination and control are the greatest priorities, hierarchy is particularly valuable. It's not surprising to find that the army is a highly hierarchical organization, for this reason.

But hierarchy also places limitations on the organization.

For a start many levels of hierarchy add a significant cost to the organization. So any organizational design should seek to minimize the number of hierarchical layers and management positions required.

The structure of a hierarchical organization can stifle creativity and initiative. It can make duties more important than goals, preventing managers from gaining the benefits of MBO and empowerment. Hierarchical organizations can also be strongly resistant to organizational change.

Do these problems invalidate what we've said so far about organizations? Fortunately not. Process design is still the best approach to making an organization efficient, and hierarchy is still the best way to control an organization. New ideas in organizational design work within these structures, rather than negate them.

Design approach: divisionalization

Divisionalization is a philosophy of organizational design in which the activities of the company are separated into highly independent business units. The organizational and operational problems are therefore pushed down into smaller and more manageable units. Meanwhile, a small central core retains financial and strategic control over the business units.

Divisionalization provides decentralized decision-making but centralized control

Divisionalization tends to shift most decision-making down to the business unit managers, who have a high degree of autonomy. But the structure also allows a very small team of senior head-office managers to control the most important decisions in the organization.

The benefits of divisionalization

Divisionalization can come about in two different ways – either by the separation of a large business in a single industry into smaller units focused on different products or markets, or by putting several diverse businesses into a single company.

For large businesses in a single industry, the divisionalized form is a trade-off. By separating the businesses, they become more manageable and can tailor strategies and culture to their individual needs. But the opportunities for operational and strategic coordination are much reduced.

Typically this kind of divisionalization occurs because there is relatively little interconnection between businesses at an operational level.

Divisionalization of a business has advantages:

- each business unit has a single manager with clear responsibility and accountability for its performance;

- business unit managers have greater incentives to perform and greater control over performance improvement;

- business units can operate as highly focused businesses with clear goals;

- decisions are made by those who know most about the business; and

- future business leaders receive excellent management training as business unit heads.

Smart people to have on your side: Alfred Sloan

General Motors
The first large company to adopt the ideas of divisionalization was General Motors in the mid-1920s. Instead of following Ford's example and creating a single large-scale organization, Sloan created different units producing different kinds of cars for different buyers. 'A car for every wallet,' said Sloan, but he might have said, 'a business unit for every customer group'. With help from Peter Drucker, he fleshed out the plan for the divisionalized corporation, which was widely adopted in the 1950s, and today dominates big business.

The role of the corporate centre

In divisionalized organizations, business are held together by a small senior management-led team that provides useful support functions to the businesses. The corporate centre:

- provides financial discipline and allocates capital to the businesses;

- provides some shared resources for all group companies (usually including: HR, IT, financial, legal, government contacts etc.) where these can be more efficiently provided at a larger scale;

- develops the company's managers;

- coordinates business unit strategy through the planning process; and

- provides a corporate brand and financial security that business partners can trust.

Does the corporate centre add value?

In the 1970s, large diversified companies were considered a great idea. The rationale was that a large diversified company could reduce its shareholders' risks by investing in many different industries. Additionally, it could be more efficient at allocating capital than the market. But as financial markets have developed, accounting standards have improved, and capital costs have fallen, many of these justifications have been negated.

In fact, multi-business companies today usually trade at a discount to the value of the individual businesses. This is because conglomeration often obscures what is actually going on in the company. By protecting business units from the fierce rigours of the market, the company often shields inefficient practices and poor strategies.

So can the value added by the corporate centre ever justify keeping businesses together?

It depends on the circumstances. In the case of a single-industry company like General Motors, the benefits are probably very large. Group businesses can share technical expertise and core competence, contacts in the retail market can be shared, managers can be developed through the company, large-scale facilities can be shared and bargaining power against suppliers can be increased.

But for a large multi-business conglomerate like Hanson, there is probably little benefit. Even super-successful conglomerate GE is coming under scrutiny from the market.

In some developing countries, political contacts can be so important to business success that it is a sufficient reason on its own to hold together large, diversified conglomerates.

Design approach: divide people into small teams

People work best in small teams.

Smart quotes

Virtually all effective teams we have met, read or heard about, or been members of have ranged between 2 and 25 people. The majority have numbered less than 10.'

Katzenbach and Smith, 'The Discipline of Teams',
HBR March–April 1993

In small teams, everyone can keep informed about what everyone else is doing. If you have 10 people in your company you have to keep in constant touch with 9 others. But if there are 100 people, you need to keep tabs on a paralysing 99 other people! The solution is to divide a company of 100 people into 10 teams of 10 – the communication needs are now 10 times smaller.

Teams also provide social benefits. Working as part of a team cooperating to achieve a common goal is a highly rewarding experience. Peer pressure tends to motivate people to work harder, while the support of a team can reduce stress.

Two kinds of teamwork are common in organizations:

- multi-functional project teams; and

- high performance work teams.

Using multi-functional teams

Multi-functional teams usually consist of specialists brought together from different parts of the organization for a specific project, enabling each to bring their particular expertise to bear on the problem at hand.

For example, a team to develop a new product could consist of a designer, a production engineer, a sales and marketing manager, a financial expert, a legal adviser and an analyst. Between them they can cover every aspect of the new product's business without protracted liaison with other parts of the organization.

In many organizations, managers have an empire mentality and resist letting their key staff work on corporate projects. Moreover, employees who operate to individual goals are less likely to want to contribute to other projects. The corporate centre must find ways to make cooperation easier. Compensation systems that favour teamwork, common company goals and manager rotation can all help to break down divisional barriers.

There is so much knowledge and skill scattered around the organization – we need to find ways to break down the barriers and get these people working together to solve the big problems.

Multi-functional teams can be useful for:

- leading change programmes;

- making a department more efficient;

- developing new products or entering new markets;

- developing company-wide strategy; and

- solving operational problems.

Using high-performance work teams

Teamwork can be used to enhance routine business processes too. Groups of workers can work together to achieve self-contained goals. Whereas an individual might normally be responsible for adding parts to a computer motherboard, a small team could take responsibility for assembling complete PCs.

A good option in high-performance work teams is to train team members to perform each other's tasks:

- work is more interesting if you can rotate roles;

- workers can cover for each other;

- collective decision-making and coordination are easier; and

- barriers are reduced and everyone is focused on common goals.

The team environment is also highly motivating and rewarding. The result of switching to a goal-oriented, team environment is often a

Smart quotes

'A demanding performance challenge … is far more important to team success than team building exercises, special initiatives or team leaders with ideal profiles.'

Katzenbach and Smith, 'The Wisdom of Teams'
(*HBR* March–April 1993)

dramatic increase in productivity. In large operations, friendly rivalry between teams also increases motivation and provides an incentive to find ways to do things better.

High performance work teams needn't be limited to the factory floor. Office workers in routine roles such as purchasing, accounting and logistics can benefit from a team structure too.

Making teams autonomous and productive

Many companies that attempt to harness the power of teamwork initially have a great deal of trouble with it. Teams rarely operate smoothly and autonomously unless they have a great deal of experience in managing themselves and working together. This takes time. Inexperienced teams need help from an experienced leader/coordinator to help them with key team needs such as decision-making, dispute resolution, administration and communication. As the team becomes more experienced, the leader's role can be progressively reduced until the team is ready to manage itself.

Smart answers to tough questions

Q: How do you create a successful team?

A: According to Katzenbach and Smith the best teams:
- establish urgency, demanding performance standards, and direction;
- select members for skill and skill potential;
- pay particular attention to first meetings and actions;
- set some clear rules of behaviour;
- set and seize upon a few immediate performance-oriented tasks and goals;
- challenge the group with fresh facts and information;
- spend lots of time together; and
- exploit the power of positive feedback, recognition and reward.

Summary of main points

- Organizational design aims to create a formal structure that makes communication easier and increases efficiency through grouping people and activities.

- A structure is chosen that is appropriate to the needs of the organization – usually this involves compromise between different kinds of organizational benefits.

- Most important is to ensure that the needs of processes critical to a company's competitive advantage are taken care of.

- Modular design and the divisionalized organization aim to simplify an organization's structure.

- Organizations can benefit from teamwork by using multi-functional project teams and high-performance work teams.

15 How to Manage Change

Is business changing faster?

No sooner have you got things figured out, than suddenly everything changes.

New products take over from old ones. Customer tastes and needs change. The economy booms and busts. New technology changes what is possible and what is needed to maintain competitive advantage. Investors are constantly on the lookout for the next big thing, seemingly ready to abandon the 'old economy'. Companies need to respond quickly if they want to keep making money.

Smart quotes

'The business world has become more competitive and more volatile. Faster technological change, greater international competition, the deregulation of markets, overcapacity in capital-intensive industries, ... and the changing demographics of the workforce are among the many factors that have contributed to this shift. Major changes are more and more necessary to survive and compete effectively in this new environment.'

John Kotter, Change Guru

Even success brings changes. With success comes growth. And with growth, companies face new organizational challenges.

So, coping with change is a critical function of management.

Even the pace of change seems to be getting quicker. It took 46 years for electricity to reach 25% of the US population, but it took the telephone only 35 years; 26 years for television, 16 years for the personal computer, 13 years for the cellular phone and only 7 years for the World Wide Web. And whereas companies used to launch a major new product every 3–5 years, they now look for new product launches every year.

The need for companies to change is radically affecting the way companies manage themselves.

Why growth can cause problems

Growth is surely a great reward for hard work. Wasn't that our aim? To find a good way to make money and leverage it to the maximum. (See Chapter 3, 'How Do Companies Create Value?') So it seems a little ungrateful to get too concerned about the *problems* growth causes:

'Problems! What problems? If only I had such problems!'

But in fact, growth can be a severe strain for many companies.

Growth is expensive. As companies grow, the amount of capital investment, training, advertising and working capital they require can quickly overtake profits and overwhelm the company.

Rapid growth can make it very hard to tell whether the underlying business is profitable and can actually produce returns. Investors in cash-burning growth companies are subject to vertigo – will the rapid rise be followed by a dramatic fall? – will it leave a white elephant with no possibility of returns?

Smart quotes

'Almost all organizations begin their lives as simple structures ... the corporate landscape is littered with the wrecks of entrepreneurial companies whose leaders encouraged growth and mass production yet could never accept the transition to bureaucratic forms of structure that these changes required.'

Henry Mintzberg, 'Organization Design' (*HBR* Jan–Feb 1981)

Even assuming companies solve their financing problems, many growing companies run into organizational problems. A flat structure with an entrepreneur at the helm serves a small venture well because it is highly flexible. But as the company grows beyond the ability of one person to manage, the need for decentralization and formal organization structures increases.

The transition is often difficult. Venture capitalists often find it simplest to replace entrepreneurial founders with experienced managers during this transition.

How to manage change

For larger companies, growth causes fewer organizational problems because a hierarchical organization tends to accommodate expansion more easily. But where small companies find they can undergo operational and strategic change relatively quickly, large companies find it far harder.

Changing a large organization can seem a daunting task. The cost of change is usually high – having to abandon and replace costly investments. And the effort involved in planning new roles for everyone is simply enormous. Senior managers must also make sure that during the transition the company continues to operate effectively.

Smart people to have on your side: Tom Peters

A new kind of excellence
Almost two decades have passed since Peters and Waterman's ground breaking *In Search of Excellence* and many of the 'excellent' companies lauded in the book have failed. Were the recommendations in the book flawed? To Peters, the conclusion is that it is not enough to be excellent at a point in time, companies must be able to keep adapting to a changing business environment.

'If the word "excellence" is to be applicable in the future, it requires wholesale redefinition. Perhaps: "Excellent firms don't believe in excellence – only in constant improvement and constant change." That is, excellent firms of tomorrow will cherish impermanence – and thrive on chaos.'

'[Resistance to change] is the most perplexing, annoying, distressing and confusing part of [change].'

Michael Hammer, *Reengineering the Corporation*

But the biggest barrier to change is more often employees' resistance to change, motivated primarily by fear and uncertainty (see box).

Smart answers to tough questions

Q: Why do people resist change?

A: Various change gurus have suggested reasons why people resist change. These include:
- fear of lower wages, more or harder work or job loss;
- difficulty in breaking habits or altering behaviours;
- lack of comprehension about why change is necessary and what is happening;
- failure to ensure that all parts of the organization are cooperating towards change;
- strong sense that change is part of a scheme by management to wrest more power and money from the rest of the organization;
- lack of control in a change that is forced upon them by others; and
- cynicism fuelled by previous failed change efforts.

Managing change is an act of leadership – it aims to make people set aside their fears and cooperate to achieve a valuable common goal.

Step 1 – Create widespread dissatisfaction with the current situation

Until people are willing to accept that change is necessary, there will be strong inertia for keeping things the way they are. Until there is a common need for change, people will look at the change process as an unnecessary imposition from head office. But without widespread support for change, a change process has very little hope of success.

Step 2 – Provide a clear vision for the new company

If the current situation represents an unsatisfactory state of affairs, then the vision must seem compellingly attractive by comparison.

A clear vision of how the company will look after the change programme gives people a sense of optimism that the company is on the road to a better future. It allows them to focus on their future role rather than on the turmoil of the change process. And it silences resistance from those still determined to fight for their own interests.

Step 3 – A detailed plan of action

In this stage all questions as to who will do what, when and how are answered. A detailed action plan reduces fear and uncertainty.

Step 4 – Set an example

Managers cannot simply ask their employees to change; they must embody these changes themselves and demonstrate that they are serious in their intention to change the company.

Symbolic gestures have a powerful impact. The CEO flying economy class, selling the Rolls Royce, and accepting a pay-cut reinforces the importance of a cost-cutting initiative.

Stories of employees exemplifying change values provide powerful examples to follow.

Senior managers should use every opportunity available to remind people of the changes they want to make – wherever possible framing strategy, policy, results and other communications in terms of the change process.

If managers won't support the change process, there should be no hesitation in firing them.

5 – Enforce the changes

The final stage of the change process ensures that people have the resources and training available to make the changes required of them.

Ideally, people should be given responsibility for making their own changes. But the company must make available all necessary resources, or risk widespread cynicism and provide excuses for not changing.

Immediately following the change process, it is necessary to control behaviours closely so that old habits do not return. Only when systems have become habitual can supervision be relaxed.

General tips for change

Throughout the process, management must:

- get complete buy-in from the senior management team;

- provide clear, honest and frequent communication to everyone;

- get everyone actively involved in the process;

- get quick, positive results to create momentum; and

- ensure that no other strategic objectives compete until the process is over.

Can companies be made more flexible?

'A few of these corporate change efforts have been very successful. A few have been utter failures. Most fall somewhere in between, with a distinct tilt toward the lower end of the scale.'

John Kotter, 'Why Transformation Efforts Fail' (*HBR* Mar–Apr 1995)

The change process described above is a radical step for a company. The great turnarounds in history, such as Lou Gerstner's effort at IBM, are rightly applauded – they are incredibly hard to pull off. Most such efforts fail. Mergers almost always require a major change initiative – but most are unsuccessful. As a result, even mergers that look great on paper often founder.

Even when they succeed, change programmes are a brutal tool – the corporate equivalent of heavy pruning. And it takes a lot of time for an organization to recover from them. Certainly one couldn't use major change initiatives on a regular basis. They are best used to make radical changes when large-scale change is unavoidable and many things can be accomplished at once.

So instead, companies should look for ways to make themselves more flexible. Can we find a way to get big company efficiency with small company flexibility?

Smart quotes

'The best companies are prepared for change because they are always preparing for it.'

Rosabeth Moss Kanter

Smart people to have on your side: Tom Peters' prescription for thriving on chaos

- Create total customer responsiveness;
- pursue fast-paced innovation;
- achieve flexibility by empowering people;
- develop leadership at all levels; and
- build systems appropriate to a changing world.

How to make infrastructure more flexible

There's a general rule: the more efficient an organization becomes, the less flexible it is. Large-scale capital investment may allow the company to obtain efficiencies, but it makes the company far harder to change.

Perhaps it is possible to get the best of both worlds. Can infrastructure be built to allow *both* scale efficiencies *and* adaptability?

One trick is to standardize and get scale economies in back-end processes where efficiency matters, and allow superficial front-end flexibility. Change then requires only front-end modifications.

For example, it might be worthwhile to have a single corporate-wide accounting system so costs are low and information can be easily exchanged. But a highly adaptable user interface would allow business units to modify the system to their own changing needs.

Factories can also be made more adaptable. Large-scale, common processes such as metal-bashing or warehousing can be designed for efficiency. Steps particular to products can be customized or be performed using flexible manufacturing techniques such as programmable robots.

How to improve people's attitude to change

If people were more amenable to change, then the effort and trauma involved in change programmes might be much reduced.

Perhaps the best hope is to involve people to a much greater degree in the company's strategy. By opening up the books to employees, the suspicions and misunderstandings that are at the root of much resistance become far less likely. If people truly understood why the company needs to change, and trusted management's motives, they might be much more enthusiastic about taking part.

For example, a cost-cutting initiative looks greedy if the company is assumed to be highly profitable. But if employees can see that the company is genuinely in dire financial difficulty due to unforeseeable market forces and that managers too are taking large salary cuts, then they may be more willing to accept them.

'Empowered' employees should also be much more willing to change. When power is based on duties, position and influence then any change is potentially threatening. But when employees have freedom to take the initiative, change is more likely to be viewed as an opportunity.

Appropriate goals can help too. If the goals are linked to the strategy, people will be willing to change *how* they meet them. On the other hand, people who remain managed by duties might be willing to change *why* they perform those duties, but not what they do.

Another way to increase people's willingness to change is to make change a natural and predictable part of their jobs. If people move jobs on a regular basis, then a corporate-wide change is just another job change. If people don't become too set in their ingrained habits, change is less likely to be feared.

Smart quotes

'People do not identify their own projects as "change". They are simply acting on their aspirations to get something done that they share and mould.'

Rosabeth Moss Kanter

Furthermore, by rotating a fair portion of employees through several parts of the company, or promoting cross-divisional projects and training, the internal barriers are broken down. Departments are less likely to defend their empires against the corporate centre. Instead, divisions are more likely to share a common culture that improves cooperation and a willingness to work for the benefit of the whole company.

Intrapreneurship: making big companies act like small entrepreneurial ventures

We want the best of both worlds: large company efficiency and small company flexibility.

If small companies can manage change better than large companies, then why not make large companies look much more like small companies?

Intrapreneurial companies try to create an internal entrepreneurial culture. They encourage good ideas and help their creators to put them into practice. The corporate centre sees itself as a venture capitalist: finding and funding ideas. Failures are acceptable and success highly rewarded.

Intrapreneurship isn't likely to work in all companies. 3M is a company whose lifeblood is creativity and innovation. In more operations-oriented companies, the value of intrapreneurship are less clear. But there are elements that can be incorporated into any company, such as the ability to rapidly assemble ad hoc project teams.

Self-cannibalization: creating constant renewal

Eventually revolutionary change will come and an innovative competitor will eat into your business. So why not be that revolutionary yourself? Why not encourage new ideas that cannibalize your own business?

Smart answers to tough questions

Q: What organizational form could cope with intrapreneurship?

A: Adhocracy – a new model for organizations.
Henry Mintzberg describes an adhocracy as 'a tremendously fluid structure, in which power is constantly shifting and coordination and control are by mutual adjustment through informal communication and interaction of competent experts.' In an adhocracy, project teams of experts are readily assembled – they are not the most efficient structures, but they are excellent at problem solving and innovation.

Perhaps the most influential example of 'the new corporate model' was the description of 3M in *In Search of Excellence*. In 3M, employees are permitted to use the company's resources to tinker with their own inventions on their own time. In fact the practice is encouraged. The company is happy to get behind a good idea on the basis of a simple one-page proposal. If a new idea can find a champion, it is pushed through development, gaining company resources and employees as it progresses. The company rewards successful ideas and teams. It also allows team members to see their work right through to implementation. Its support for great ideas makes the company appealing and rewarding for employees and highly innovative. And its ability to assemble ad hoc teams is widely admired.

We can't rely on competitors to push us forward – we need to be driven to constant improvement from within.

The result would be an internally driven spiral of constant improvement. Confronted with a company willing to compete with itself, competitors would never be able to keep up with the rapid pace of innovation.

GE's 'destroyyourbusiness.com' initiative is a great example of self-cannibalization. Rather than wait for competition to force GE to adopt Internet technologies, each business was challenged to create its own Internet revolution.

Self-organization

What if companies could re-organize themselves in response to environmental and strategic pressures? What if every part of the organization had the ability to see the strategic needs and organize itself accordingly without any direct intervention by senior corporate managers? Change wouldn't require expensive initiatives: it would be an ongoing, organic process. Employee resistance wouldn't be an issue because employees would be driving the changes at every level.

But is this fantasy possible? What does a company need in order to organize itself?

Self-organizing systems require each part of the organization to:

- have a clear goal to work towards;

- get access to or create the resources and support services that it needs to meet its goal; and

- find and effectively communicate with parts of the organization whose cooperation it needs.

In fact, all organizations *do* meet these criteria to some extent and all exhibit some level of self-organization.

People try to mould their organization to let them do what they need to do.

For example, very few new organizational structures meet all the needs of all of the parts of the organization first up. In most companies, informal processes and communications develop to compensate. If you can't get the information you need through formal channels, why not call up someone you know and try to get hold of it another way?

Companies tend to get more efficient over time as they compensate for weaknesses in their formal structures. No wonder management-led

How can
we help the
organization
shape itself?

change initiatives are so traumatic. Not only is the company's formal structure being changed, but the organization also needs to learn how to get things done all over again.

Clearer goals would help companies self-organize in the correct way – then people could more easily work out what they needed. Decentralization of power and greater autonomy would help to accelerate change – people could more easily get the resources they need. In short, the answer is more MBO and empowerment.

Summary of main points

- Change is becoming more important in business.

- However, major change initiatives are costly and traumatic mainly owing to internal employee resistance.

- A process for accomplishing major change focuses on breaking down employee resistance.

- There are ways to make companies more flexible, by:

  - setting clearer strategic goals; and
  - increasing employee empowerment.

16 Keeping Track of the Money

The role of accounting in providing management information

In this chapter we're going to learn a little bit of accounting.

'Aaagggh!'

Managers play the game; the accountants keep the score.

Hey – we've avoided it for fifteen chapters already.

For some reason, accounting inspires dread amongst otherwise rational business people. But really there's nothing to fear. When we're through you'll ask yourself what all the fuss was about. And those of you who think you can find your way around a balance sheet, you'd better stick around too, because we're about to discover there's more to it than that.

Are we actually making money?

No businessperson is going to get far without at least a basic grasp of accounting. You might have heard that 'accounting is the language of business'. Well, sort of. It's really just a way of keeping track of the money. And if you recall, that's how we got into this business – money. So you'd better be able to tell how much money you're making. And a good understanding of your accounts can tell you a great deal about where you are making money, where to look for more and even give early warning of problems.

What exactly are profits?

Profit accounting has been around for centuries. Not surprising really, since in essence profit is the simplest idea imaginable in business. It costs you $6 to make a paper aeroplane. You sell it to the big kid on the playground for $10. Congratulations! You just made $4 of profit. About enough for about a dozen gobstoppers. Kid's play!

Profit accounting is just the same process on a much bigger scale. You buy 100 second-hand Boeing 747s for $4 billion, and sell them for $5 billion. Hey, you're a billionaire!

But reality is never quite so simple. Because, at the end of all that, you almost certainly won't have $1 billion in cash. So what went wrong? We'd better delve a little deeper.

Calculating profit

The matching principle

At any given time, there's a lot going on in a company. We're paying suppliers, incurring production costs and buying new equipment. Meanwhile, we've sold most of our goods on credit and we're still waiting for the cash to come in. Luckily most of our materials have been bought on credit too, because until the cash arrives we can't pay our bills. It's all a rather confusing mess – cash is flowing in and out like water through a sieve. To work out what profits we're earning we'd better find some rules to help us see what's going on.

The most important rule for sorting through this confusion is called the 'matching principle'.

With the matching principle, we record all of the costs and revenues of a particular product sale at the same time. That way we know whether, after all the costs we incurred along the way, we've made a profit or not. Usually we record profits at the moment the customer agrees to buy the product.[1]

Of course, the matching principle is just a convenient fiction. We almost certainly incurred the costs long before the sale – some when we bought the materials, some during production and some when transporting and storing the finished products. Equally, at the time of sale, we probably won't have received money from the customer yet.

But imagine if we didn't use the matching principle – at any given time we've probably spent more money on making products than we've so far got from selling them, so it would look like we were doing badly, when in fact we're making big profits on every sale.

Working capital

So what do we do with all those costs that we haven't matched up yet?

We call these 'working capital' (the name comes from the fact that we need to finance these costs in order to operate) and record them on an account called the balance sheet.

It's worth watching working capital, because growing companies especially can find themselves running short of cash even when they're making a profit. So make sure that cash + inventories (materials and products yet to be sold) + receivables (what's owed *to you*) is always greater than your creditors (what you owe *to others*).

'Fixed assets' and 'depreciation'

Technology often means buying expensive bits of machinery in order to produce goods. These huge purchases can't be matched to a single sale. Instead, the cost is shared out between all the goods the machine helps to produce. If a \$1,000,000 packaging machine is expected to contribute towards the production of 200,000,000 cans of beer in its lifetime, then 0.5c of the total cost of the machine is allocated to each can of beer.

This allocation is called depreciation. That is because the cost remaining to be allocated is recorded on the balance sheet and depreciated by 0.5c on every sale of a can of beer.

How to deal with 'overhead' costs

Some costs cannot easily be matched to individual products. The cost of managers or of interest payments on debt and many other 'overhead' costs are simply charged as they are incurred.

The purpose of the 'balance sheet'

The balance sheet keeps a record of everything the company owns, owes or is owed. It records the state of play at a particular moment in time.

The balance sheet is so called because it always balances: what you own and are owed (your assets) always balance what you owe (your liabilities).

How can this be? Personal experience tells us we can quite easily find ourselves owning assets without owing money to anyone.

If we purchase an asset with cash all we are really doing is shifting from one asset (cash) to another, so the balance sheet still balances.

When we owe money it is usually because we borrowed to buy assets or materials that we own – so an increase in what we owe is generally balanced by an increase in what we own. And when we are owed money, it is because we have given away goods of that value – so the increase in what we are owed balances the decrease in what we own.

But if we make a profit on a sale, things don't seem to balance – when we sell a good for a profit, we expect to receive more money than we bought it for. Similarly we sometimes incur costs and receive nothing tangible in return for them.

To ensure that everything continues to balance, we record profits on the balance sheet, too. Note that to keep the balance sheet in balance, profits must be a liability – we owe it to someone! Surely that's crazy; the whole point is to make profits, profits are good, no?

Well, the first thing to remember is that profits are a fiction – what we really want is hard cash and that is an asset. Profits tell us how much cash we will earn when all the timing differences have finally sorted themselves out. Profits aren't good until they turn into cold hard cash.

The other thing to remember is that the company is owned by its shareholders – everything the company owns really belongs to the shareholders. Profit tells us how much more assets the company has accumulated (eventually to be turned into cash) and hence how much more the company owes to its shareholders.

The example below lists some activities of a start-up company to demonstrate these principles. If you still don't believe balance sheets must balance or don't understand why they should, you might want to work through the example carefully.

Action taken	Impact on assets (We own/are owed)	Impact on liabilities (We owe)
Shareholder invests $1500	Cash +$1500	Investors' funds[a] +$1500
Buy a machine for $1000 that will manufacture 100 products during its life	Cash – $1000 Fixed assets +$1000	
Run up $200 of costs producing 2 products	Inventories[b] +$200	Supplier creditors[d] +$200
Pay $150 to suppliers	Cash -$150	Supplier creditors -$150
Depreciate machine by $20 in producing goods	Fixed assets – $20 Inventories[b] + $20	
Sell 1 finished product for $150 ($40 profit)	Inventories[b] – $110 Receivables[c] +$150	Profits earned[a] + $40
Receive $140 in cash from customer	Receivables – $140 Cash +$140	
Pay managers $10	Cash – $10	Profits earned[e] – $10
Pay $10 in dividends to investors from profits	Cash – $10	Investors funds[a] – $10

Notes
[a] Investors' funds and Profits earned are both owed to shareholders and in practice are recorded in the same balance sheet account.
[b] Costs attributed to a product before it is sold are recorded as inventories.
[c] Revenue, where the cash is not yet received, is recorded as a receivable.
[d] Money owed to suppliers.
[e] Overhead costs are taken directly from profits.

After all that, here's what the balance sheet looks like:

Assets (We own/we are owed)	$	Liabilities (We owe)	$
Cash	470	Investors funds[a]	1520
Fixed Assets	980	Supplier creditors[b]	50
Inventories[b]	110		
Receivables[b]	10		
TOTAL	1570	TOTAL	1570

Notes
[a] Of which Profits retained (Profits earned less Dividends paid) = $20
[b] Working capital items

At the end of the day, the company made an operating profit of $30, of which $10 was returned to the investor as a dividend payment. The company now has $470 in cash, a machine whose depreciated value is $980, $110 of inventories (unfinished and unsold product) and is owed $10 by customers – total assets of $1570. Its liabilities are also $1570, of which $1520 is owed to its investor and $50 is owed to suppliers.

The Profit-and-Loss account records how the profits were earned:

Revenues	$150
Cost of goods sold	($110)
Overhead costs	($10)
Profits earned	$30
Dividends paid	($10)
Profits retained (change in Investors funds)	$20

Smart quotes

'The primary purpose of financial statements is to show the underlying economic performance of a company. The balance sheet provides a snapshot, at a moment in time, of the assets, liabilities and capital of the business; and the income statement, or profit-and-loss account, shows the difference between total revenues and total expenses.'

The Economist 4 May 2002

How to calculate how much cash has been used or earned

Cash is King.

Ultimately cash matters. Profits are useful because they make it easier to see the true picture of whether the company is making money or not. But investors will be repaid in cash, interest payments are in cash, suppliers want cash and employees are paid in cash. Companies get into financial difficulties when they run out of cash, not profits. So somewhere along the line, you need to know how much cash you're generating too.

The cash flow ought to be the easiest thing to calculate – just look at what cash enters and leaves the company's balance sheet. But investors also like to see how the activities of the business, as described in the profit-and-loss account and the balance sheet, match up to the cash movements. Remember that working capital tracks the timing differences between earning cash and profits, so we ought to be able to work from one to the other.

Smart quotes

'Only earnings increases that are associated with improved long-term cash flow will increase share prices.'

Copeland et al., Valuation

Cashflow from Operations – Direct Calculation		Cashflow from Operations – From Other Accounts	
Cash receipts	$140	Operating Profit	+ $30
Cash payments	($160)	Add back of non-cash costs included in profits (depreciation)	+ $20
		Change in Working Capital* Inventories Receivables Supplier Creditors	- $110 - $10 + $50
CASH FROM OPERATIONS Assets Acquired Cash from funding Dividends paid	($20) ($1000) $1500 ($10)	CASH FROM OPERATIONS	($20)
TOTAL CASHFLOW	$470		

Note

* Receivables indicates profit that has been recorded but no cash has been received, so the higher the receivables, the worse the cash position relative to the profit position. Similarly inventories – cash has been paid but no cost has been recorded on the profit account. Supplier creditors are the reverse – we have recorded the cost of the goods, but not yet paid cash, so the cash position is better than the profit position.

How managers use accounting to get more detailed information

Managers use accounts to keep track, too. But usually they need more detailed information than overall corporate accounts provide. For investors, it is enough to know how much profit is being made and that the business has enough cash to get by. But managers want to keep track of the profits made by each department, product, customer group

Where are we making our money?

and activity. By doing so, they can see what's working, what needs attention and what should be stopped.

In principle, management accounts are easy to produce by separating each accounting record into department, product etc. For example, a beverage manufacturer might want to separate accounts into carbonated versus juices; or US market versus overseas markets; or bottling operations versus syrup manufacture.

The point of management accounting is to help you answer questions about the business.

The accounting system can also be used to track extra information useful to managers, such as number of units produced or sold.

But it's not quite that easy. The biggest problem comes with deciding how to allocate shared costs that relate to more than one activity. For example, a single machine may be used to produce several different products.

How you deal with shared costs depends on what questions you are asking.

Management accounting: the 'constraint costing' approach to fixed shared costs

At any given point in time, fixed-cost resources that are not being fully utilized can be considered to have no additional usage cost – any additional contribution is beneficial to the company. This greatly simplifies things – we don't need to allocate these shared costs at all. All we need to worry about is whether producing a given product will make a positive contribution to help cover these fixed shared costs.

But when a fixed-cost resource is fully utilized, it is very costly to use. Using the resource requires the company to free up capacity by producing less of other products – when those products' entire profit contribution is lost.

Constraint costing measures the costs of these limited resources. It allows the business to make the best short-term decisions about resource usage. A product that cannot contribute more than its constraint costs shouldn't be produced.

Constraint costing represents the true economic cost of the resource at a point in time. But it is not the most useful measure for making long-term decisions. The first problem is that utilization (and hence constraint costs) tends to fluctuate greatly, making it hard to determine profitability over any long period of time. Also, over time, companies can easily relieve resource limitations through new investment, so constraint costs do not represent costs over the long-term.

Management accounting: the 'activity based costing' approach to variable shared costs

'The cost that matters for competitiveness and profitability is the cost of the total process, and that is what activity-based costing records and makes manageable.'

Peter Drucker

When the cost of a shared resource varies greatly depending on what is being produced, shared costs should be allocated to products in order to get a clear picture of whether the product is profitable to the company as a whole.

Activity based costing (ABC) is the best way to do this. Shared costs are allocated according to an assessment of what activities cause them to be incurred.

To illustrate, let's say that the costs of a machine are being allocated between two different products. One product uses up only a little machine time and the other a great deal. Since the cost of this particular machine depends mainly on running time, its cost is allocated to the products according to how much time they use.

Back-office costs, on the other hand, might be allocated according to the number of invoices sent out for each product.

Smart things to say

It's no good measuring financial performance at the top level only – we need to know who is making money and who isn't at every level of the company.

In the long-term, almost all costs are variable – i.e. they depend on the volume of business in some way. Therefore ABC gives a good reflection of the long-run cost to the business of each product. Long-term decisions about which products to focus on and whether to expand resources are best made using ABC.

Managing people to profit measures

So we now have a method for calculating the profit of any division, product, machine or activity. We can use this information to help manage people. If we know the profit impact of every employee action, we can use this information to ensure that people make the right decisions, and even measure each individual's contribution to corporate profits.

Measuring profits at such a low level ought to be of great practical benefit. If people know what profit each of their actions will contribute,

Smart people to have on your side: John Humble

Putting MBO into practice
John Humble is a British consultant who during the 1960s and 1970s attempted to turn Peter Drucker's ideas on MBO into a practical system of management. Humble's aim was to create a system in which organizational goals could be translated into personal goals, so that individuals could be held personally accountable for company performance. In practice, it amounted to setting measurable financial targets for business unit managers.

then they will always know what to do to act in the best interests of the company. And they can be held accountable for the actions they take.

Profit measures tend to focus attention on the measurable and the short-term. Intangibles such as 'customer satisfaction' tend to get lost in a systematic approach to profit accountability, so that customer value is destroyed and the company may suffer in the long-term.

Are we ignoring important aspects of the business because we can't measure them?

Profit-based goals tend not to be particularly motivating either, but this can be dealt with through incentive payments or better still, an employee share ownership programme.

Nevertheless, it is useful for managers to understand how individual activities contribute to overall profits and many schemes for analysing activities in fine detail are used in business.

'Shareholder Value' as a performance measure

Another question worth asking is whether profit is actually what we should be measuring. Investors care about profit – they want to be sure that their investment is making money.

'Creditors and shareholders expect to be compensated for the opportunity cost of investing their funds.'

Copeland et al.,
Valuation

But is an annual profit of $1 million a good thing? Well, it rather depends on how much you invested. If you invested $10 million, then 10% is a pretty good return. But if you invested $100 million then you'd have done better by putting the money in the bank.

Shareholder Value accounting allows companies to take the investors' view of the world into account. Instead of managing to profit, companies should be managing to what really matters to investors: Shareholder Value.

Shareholder Value is a profit calculation that includes an explicit cost for the return that investors expect. If profits are below the required return level, then Shareholder Value is negative. If profits exceed the required return, then Shareholder Value is positive.

Is all our capital earning a sufficient return?

If, for example, the required return is 10% and the capital invested is $10 million, then as far as the investor is concerned, they have only made money if the profits are at least 10% – i.e. $1 million. Anything less and the investor will be looking for an alternative investment pretty quickly.

We should measure our success in the same terms as our investors – we need to be aware of what capital costs.

When analysing the profit of individual activities, Shareholder Value is vastly superior to profit analysis, since it also accounts for how much investment capital different activities tie up.

In a company, some profitable activities use very little capital and therefore provide huge returns, while others are real capital guzzlers and don't provide decent returns. Clearly, companies should be able to distinguish between the two.

Smart answers to tough questions

Q: What returns do investors require?

A: Just as in any other market, the price of capital (the required rate of return) depends on supply and demand. In this case, the market is the whole country's investors and businesses.

The *supply* of capital is the amount of money in the economy available for investment. It depends mostly on the amount individuals choose to invest[2] rather than spend in a given year. The amount of money people invest depends on the rate of return they get from investing – the higher the rate of return, the more tempting it is to invest now so that more can be spent next year. (Witness the surge in share investing during the economic boom.) When the rate of return is low, you might as well spend the money now rather than wait to spend the same amount next year.

The *demand* for capital is all the investment projects in the economy that need funding. As the required rate of return increases, only the most profitable ventures can satisfy investors, so demand falls.

The market rate of return is the rate at which supply matches demand. Usually the required rate of return is around 4% plus price inflation.[3]

But that is not the end of the story. Investors also demand a higher return if they have to take a risk. But interestingly, it is not the risk of an individual investment that matters. Only the extent to which the company's fortunes depend on the economy as a whole![4] In general an investor can invest in several companies and some will do well and others badly, but overall, the good and the bad will average out. But in an economic downturn, all the companies will do badly at the same time, probably at exactly the time the investor is most in need of cash. So the more exposed the company is to the economy as a whole, the greater the additional return that will be demanded.

Typically, shareholders demand a risk premium of around 6–8%.

Return requirements on bank debt are rather lower. Firstly, because there is far less risk – debt payments are the same every year regardless of how well the company performs; the only risk is if the company is in such bad financial trouble that it can't pay. And secondly, the government actually helps out with paying debt – companies calculate their taxes after the cost of debt so that the more interest they pay, the less tax they pay.[5]

When inflation is low (around 2%) then for a normal, rich-country company that's not in financial difficulty, the company's required rate of return is usually around 10%. If you're just estimating, 10% is a convenient figure that probably won't be too far wrong.

'A dollar today is worth more than a dollar tomorrow.'

Brearly and Myers, *Principles of Corporate Finance*

Managing using 'value-based management'

Value-based management (VBM) is the name for a management approach that uses Shareholder Value. Its main tool is the use of Share-

Smart people to have on your side: Alfred Rappaport and G. Bennet Stuart

Popularizers of value-based management
During the 1980s and 1990s, value-based management started to gain popularity amongst large companies. The idea was appealing – by understanding the 'drivers' of financial value in the business, each part of the company could be set goals to enhance the company's value. But most managers feared that accurately measuring a company's value, or worse yet, identifying what drives it, would be too difficult in practice. Rappaport, a lecturer at the Kellogg Graduate School of Management and Stuart, founder of management consultancy Stern Stuart, provided simple concepts, procedures and tools to make value-based management work in practice.

holder Value instead of profits as a basis for goal setting, measurement and rewards. But it also encompasses the discipline of using Shareholder Value in planning, investor relations and decision-making.

Does everyone understand how to create shareholder value?

Companies such as PepsiCo have found VBM a useful tool for instilling financial discipline in their decision-making and planning.

But as with using any system of financial goals, it is probably best to supplement VBM with goals better suited to motivation and long-term efficient customer value creation. And indeed some versions of VBM

Smart quotes

'When VBM is implemented well, the corporate receives tremendous benefit ... It works ... Yet VBM is not without pitfalls ... A value-based manager [should be] as interested in the subtleties of organizational behaviour as in using valuation for a performance metric and decision-making tool.'

Copeland *et al.*, *Valuation*

do try to include long-term future performance rather than just one-year returns.

Summary of main points

- Profit accounting is an important tool for working out what is going on in companies.

- Because the timing of cash receipts and payments in a company is so variable, the main task of profit accounting is to match up all the revenues and profits from the same sale.

- Managers can use the principles of profit accounting to determine the profitability of individual activities, although how they deal with shared costs depends on the nature of the costs and on what decisions they are looking to make.

- Since investors care about returns rather than profits, a useful management measure is Shareholder Value – profit less an additional charge for the cost of using investors' capital.

Notes

1   Some industries such as construction, banking and insurance have slightly different rules about what constitutes a sale owing to the nature of the products they sell.

2   Savings put in pensions and bank accounts are also considered to be investments because, in both cases, the money is ultimately invested in the market by the pension fund or bank.

3   Inflation matters a great deal, of course: if you could buy $100 worth of goods this year then there is no point investing if you

can't afford the same goods next year. If your investment gives you $110, but the goods now cost $120 you are actually worse off.

4   Seriously. Investors may discount the profit forecasts of risky tech companies, but they don't demand a higher rate of return from them.

5   In some countries, shareholders also receive some tax relief on dividend payments from shares.

17 The Future of Business

How business will evolve in the future

The seeds of the future are sown in the present.

The future will be both more similar and more different than we can imagine.

Business will always be about efficient customer value creation. But how business goes about it is changing. Just as our post-industrial times have heralded ideas like 'empowerment' and MBO, which are slowly percolating into the business community, we can expect that many of today's cutting edge ideas will in their turn find themselves consigned to the out-box of history. This chapter will hopefully give you an idea of some of the trends nudging their way into sight, from which tomorrow's ideas are likely to emerge.

Some of the trends listed below will no doubt be proven unimportant or temporary. Others yet unseen will become highly significant. There are certainly plenty of people willing to give their opinion on the future. This chapter describes some of the more considered of these opinions. But we can be certain of only one thing: the future will, as ever, surprise us.

Business trend: the ascent of knowledge workers

The increasing sophistication of business means that almost all workers need more specialist training for their jobs. Where once unskilled factory workers dominated urban employment, they are fast becoming a minority.

A quick glance at the jobs people do today reveals the extent of this transformation. Engineers, technicians, trained managers and marketing and finance professionals dominate many companies. Elsewhere in the economy, technicians, computer programmers and other 'knowledge workers' similarly dominate. These jobs may not require constant intellectual creativity – the jobs are often *doing* jobs rather than purely *thinking* jobs. But what characterizes them is that they require substantial training, expert knowledge and developed skills. Knowledge workers need to make judgement calls about what they do and how they do it.

We have already started to see the impact on management. It is no longer sufficient to give people duties to carry out. If they are to use their judgement appropriately, they need to understand their organization's goals and be given the autonomy and responsibility to act as they see fit. Increasingly, work will consist of projects rather than management-led duties.

But can the educational system provide enough of the right kinds of skilled employees? The likely answer is no – not without major change. Some jobs, such as computer programming, have serious problems finding sufficient skilled workers.

It seems that the solution will be for companies to take more responsibility for training their staff. Some companies already have 'corporate universities' for skills training and the trend is likely to continue. In addition, companies will need to think more carefully about career path development for their workers.

Smart people to have on your side: Peter Drucker

Management in the 21st century
Drucker's vision of the future (in his book *Management Challenges for the 21st Century*) is based in the demographic and management trends taking place today. The aging of the population will have implications that businesses cannot ignore. Leading change will become an ever more important part of businesses. Companies will have to learn to cope with the breakdown of international and political barriers. The vast increase in information availability presents new opportunities as well as new challenges – 'Companies have to learn to organize information as their key resource'.

But most important is the increasing importance of 'knowledge workers' – workers for whom specialist knowledge is a key component of their jobs. The challenge of improving knowledge worker productivity will be very different from that of improving manual worker productivity. New organizational forms will be needed in which they can effectively contribute, since they are no longer subordinates, but 'associates'. And given the increased freedom that entails, how can individuals develop their skills and abilities? And how can the organization be effectively led?

'The most valuable assets of a 20th century company were its production equipment. The most valuable asset of a 21st century institution, whether business or nonbusiness, will be its knowledge workers and their productivity.'

The rise of contractors

Knowledge workers might become too specialized for a single company to use effectively. As a result, more are likely to work as contractors or consultants, or to work on projects for many different companies over their careers.

Already, skilled temporary agencies are growing fast. Could we ever reach a point where companies consist entirely of groups of skilled contractors?

Perhaps we are getting closer, as technology reduces some of the problems of coordination and management, which traditional companies solve by hiring permanent staff in a permanent location.

Big changes in the management of companies would be required to cope with large groups of contractors.

Business trend: the connected world

Communication, whether in the form of the Internet or cellular phones, is already making a real difference in the way we live our lives. It is also likely to have a significant impact on company operations.

The Internet represents a technological change on the scale of electricity or the telephone – we've barely begun to see its impact.

Companies will be able to communicate with each other far more easily. The Internet provides a common standard for cheaply exchanging information.

The biggest changes are happening behind the scenes of heavy industry. Business-to-business exchanges, purchasing, supplier and customer management are all being transformed. The cost savings are likely to be very large indeed.

Smart quotes

'Free trade offers all countries, both rich and poor, chances to gain by specializing in what they do best. Globalization arguably comes down to nothing more than allowing this specialization to happen.'

Micklethwait and Wooldridge, *A Future Perfect*
paraphrasing the free-trade economist David Ricardo

Equally importantly, cooperation between companies is greatly enhanced. One example is that factories can get instant access to their parts-suppliers systems – allowing suppliers to predict demand better, reducing supply delays and stock-outs while reducing inventory. Customers can get instant information on what is available and what constraints their suppliers face. The result may be that several companies can operate together just as efficiently as if they were all part of the same organization.

And of course, the Internet (and in future, 3G cellular phones) allows companies to interact with their customers in new ways. More informed customer decision-making will change the role of marketing from selling to providing information. New ways to offer services to customers will be possible, going far beyond the glorified mail order we've seen so far.

We've barely even begun to see all the potential benefits from the Internet yet.

Business trend: managers without borders

The world economy is globalizing and has been for some time. Free trade is benefiting rich countries and poor countries alike.

For countries, there are dangers too – cultures are homogenising, many countries risk being stuck in a small number of commodity industries where they are frighteningly at the mercy of global pricing fluctuations.

But on the whole, there are mainly benefits from trade – foreign companies offer capital, technology and training that help to boost efficiency in the local economy. Often this far outweighs the direct benefits of trade.

But surely this is old hat. And what impact does it have on business?

The big change is that a worldwide business community is starting to develop. Companies that have operated in only one country, or separately in many, are increasingly finding that the barriers between countries are falling. Most businesses are just beginning to learn how to cope with the flows of people between countries, how to build corporate cultures that can cope with national differences, and how to do business in multiple languages simultaneously.

> The barriers between countries are falling – managers need to learn how to think and act globally, even if they never leave their offices.

A worldwide business community means being able to combine skills and expertise that may be geographically far apart. It means being able to quickly get to grips with the local business conditions. It means being able to use the best practices, best resources and best ideas from anywhere in the world. And it all requires a radically more cosmopolitan outlook than most businesses are used to.

Finally, it means that companies need to benchmark themselves not just against their local competitors, but with the best companies in the world.

Companies will need to learn how to meet these new challenges. Managers need to be open to doing business in alien cultures, foreign languages and new business environments, even if they never leave their offices.

But history gives cause for caution. The breaking down of national barriers is always a cause for political friction. The transformations that globalization catalyses lead to losers as well as winners; and foreigners are easily blamed for domestic ills. There have been other periods of major global expansion – they almost all ended badly.

Smart quotes

'The more successful globalization becomes, the more it seems to whip up its own backlash.'

Micklethwait and Wooldridge, *A Future Perfect*

Business trend: socially responsible management

In theory, companies' only responsibility is to their shareholders. Governments may place restrictions on behaviour when it is in the public interest to do so, and competition provides pressure for efficient value creation, but the focus of business needs only to be on producing profits for shareholders. So the trend toward socially responsible business suggests that something is wrong with this model.

Increasingly, workers and customers are expecting companies to behave in a socially responsible manner. Perhaps this reflects the ever-larger role companies are playing in our social lives – for example, corporate marketing is increasingly defining rather than responding to popular culture. Workers are showing that their company's effect on society matters to them, and they are increasingly willing to blow the whistle on company practices they disapprove of. Consumers are increasingly engaging in activism against multinational corporations to pursue political ends.

Social responsibility matters to us, because it matters to our workers, customers and shareholders. Ultimately, our success depends on society's support of the service we provide.

Socially responsible institutional investors are even emerging, demonstrating that financial returns are not the only things that matter to all shareholders.

Whatever the causes, the trend towards socially responsible management demonstrates that business is starting to take some responsibility for social wellbeing. If the trend continues, a new balance will need to be struck between government and business. It may no longer be

What social
obligations does
our company
have?

sufficient for companies to pursue return on shareholders' investment as their primary goal, but also return on social responsibility. It will require new approaches to performance measurement and new kinds of strategy to deliver it.

In particular, at a time when companies are decentralizing, there is also greater pressure for managers to detect and punish unethical employee behaviour.

For companies, there may be many additional costs associated with taking on social responsibility, but if real value is being provided, then there is always a benefit to be gained for the company.

Business trend: an end to work?

'In the future, machines will do all the work while we enjoy the results.'

Ian Pearson, Futurologist

Over the last 150 years, the product of one hour of labour has increased tenfold. Will it ever reach a point where labour is actually unnecessary? And can our growth in prosperity continue forever?

For the most part, in manufacturing industries, machines already do much of the actual work, while people provide ideas and management.

Assuming the trend continues, it is worth asking what happens in a society in which no one *has* to work. How do people obtain their share of the wealth? And what role will business play in society?

Current societal organization may prove insufficient. In today's labour-dominated economy, the biggest limited resource is labour, so everyone can share in the wealth by working for a salary. Instead, in a work-free world, the resource owners will get richer and richer, while most of the rest of the population will get poorer. To maintain social equilibrium, governments may be forced to redistribute ownership or wealth in more aggressive ways. There is a risk that this will reduce business opportunity.

While it is easy to see productivity improvements in manufacturing reaching their logical conclusion, will the same be true of services? In many western countries, manufacturing efficiency gains have simply led to a much bigger service sector. Many service jobs are highly labour intensive and resist attempts to improve efficiency. It is a notable irony that computer programming is stubbornly labour intensive. But elsewhere in our urban lives we are increasing labour intensive services – tourism, call-centres, fast-food restaurants, construction and even management. Until we find a way to make these far more efficient, little will really change. For business, finding ways to deliver services more efficiently will be a key challenge.

If we ever do reach a work-free world, the role of companies is likely to change dramatically. Companies will become less about people and processes than about ideas and resources. New management processes will be necessary to cope with companies that run with few people, all of whom having a creative rather than an operational role to play. Which brings us more or less full circle, as these are precisely the management challenges that knowledge workers are already bringing to management.

Summary of main points

Trends that will affect business in future:

● increased autonomy, project-work and contractors;

● more meaningful work and better opportunities for development;

● substantial new efficient customer value creation opportunities from new communication technologies;

- increasing need to manage across market, country, language and cultural boundaries;

- social responsibility as a company objective and greater control over unethical behaviour in the workplace; and

- new ways to make labour-intensive services more efficient.

PART III

Achieving Personal Success

18 How to Achieve Personal Success in Business

Playing the political game

'Man is a political animal' according to Aristotle. And nowhere more so than at work. In the corporate village, employees do battle for influence and the favour of their managers. Success is rapid promotion to the ranks of power and control over a large empire of employees and corporate resources. Failure is a dead-end career. With the stakes so high, is it any wonder that companies are a hotbed of political intrigue?

To succeed, you need to be popular, win visible victories and eliminate the competition. Just like success in business, success in politics comes from successful tactics and strategy.

Strategists work on building their reputations. They position themselves to get the jobs that lead to glory and avoid projects that are too risky or too hard. They build up networks of influence to be cashed in when the time is right.

Tacticians accumulate small victories, taking every opportunity to exploit the mistakes of their competitors, wherever possible setting them up for visible and humiliating failures. Great tacticians know how to distance themselves from disaster and maximize the glory from successes (however tenuous their connection to them).

Information is a key weapon, and its lack, an exposure to humiliation. Facts are both friends and enemies – and are most effective as weapons when they are vague enough to suit a beneficial interpretation.

Politics is a game won by the crafty and the strong, the talented and the skilful. Politicians know how to 'spin' perception in their favour. They must be able to read the political landscape – to understand how people behave and, especially, what their weaknesses are.

Politicians need to be superhumanly disciplined – the manipulations of politicians will offend if they are detected. Good timing is essential.

But who can control their greed all the time, when even small misjudgements can lead to failure? When trust is an essential tool for business leadership, even the smallest slip can be fatal. And there's always a better politician about ...

And the time consumed by politicking makes it harder to do anything productive. And at the end of it all, you realize that your machinations have far less impact on your destiny than you might prefer to believe.

So, while politics comes naturally, it is very risky strategy. All but the most skilled politicians would be well advised to avoid it.

Is politics all bad?

Is all political behaviour to be avoided then?

Not at all. Many 'political' activities are actually good for the company. Building up networks of allies is valuable to the company because communication is enhanced. Reciprocation and generosity give people an incentive to help each other out. And influence and popularity are powerful forces for communicating positive messages around the company. Without some skill in influence, leadership is much harder. And nurturing a good reputation is critical if strangers in a large organization are to trust you.

Undermining your peers is clearly not a productive behaviour. Yet some good-natured competition can be motivating. Dishonesty and secrecy are destructive – information that could be useful to others must be shared. But there's a limit to how honest you might want to be. There's no point making enemies. In business you have a task to achieve and everyone needs to work together. You can't afford the luxury of isolating and hurting people just because they infuriate you. It's tough not to respond emotionally, but professionalism is a virtue that should be respected in any organization.

Smart quotes

'While it's undeniably true that there are unprincipled players in the world of office politics and that there are tactics and strategies for office politics that can be downright immoral, it's also possible to be active and effective in your organization's political environment in ways that are principled and ethical.'

Michael and Deborah Dobson, *Enlightened Office Politics*

Killer questions

Am I acting in the company's best interests? Will I be embarrassed if my behaviour becomes common knowledge?

This is not a book on corporate ethics. The decision is yours. Are you prepared to go beyond the beneficial aspects of positive interpersonal behaviour and pursue your own self-interest at the expense of the company? Are you willing to encourage others to do the same? Can you accept the risks of getting caught out?

The straight-shooter approach to political success

For non-politicians, poor politicians and idealists, there is fortunately an alternative path to success. You can win by refusing to play seedy political games: get a reputation as a 'straight-shooter'.

Make it a pleasure for people to work with you. Be an earnest, loyal, hard worker whose main concern is the welfare of the company.

Smart answers to tough questions

Q: How can you avoid manipulative politics?

A: Get a reputation as a 'straight-shooter':
- primary focus is on company and team goals rather than personal achievements. Value team contribution over individualism;
- back up assertions with facts and hard data not opinion, hearsay and feelings;
- value logical argument over consensus or bullying;
- value honesty and openness;
- place a high priority on learning and development;
- be willing to sacrifice short-term glory for long-term success; and
- provide regular feedback and updates to keep others informed of their progress.

Use hard data and clear logical arguments. And avoid opinion and supposition – opinions should always be backed up with evidence, if only to protect you against those who would undermine you.

'Always tell the truth, then you don't have to remember what you've said.'

Mark Twain

Build a team of talented straight-shooters around you.

Even successful straight-shooters need tangible results. That means going for easy victories wherever possible. Play to your strengths and make success easy. Attempt problems you know you can solve until your reputation is beyond doubt.

Smart things to say

Good decisions are made on the basis of hard data not opinion and hearsay.

Become known as the pinch-hitter – the one who can be turned to for a reliable, strong, effective performance for the really big issues.

How to manage your personal brand

Just like products, people in organizations need to summarize their key strengths so managers know when to use them. You need a brand.

Ideally, your brand matches the areas most important to the company's strategy. But don't go beyond what you can succeed at.

Everyone has a reputation, so it's better to have a good one.

The straight-shooter brand is a valuable one. But it helps to be more specific. Build real expertize in a few related areas and sell that expertize to others. Work on projects that help reinforce your brand. Manage your boss – get him to delegate to you the jobs you want. Try to get some easy wins in early to help you build your brand.

Admitting weaknesses can actually be a good thing – it accentuates your strengths, deflects charges of arrogance, and helps you avoid projects that won't help you build your brand. (A brand must know what it isn't!)

What are my
strengths?
Where can I
excel?

Get really good at doing what you claim to be good at!

When necessary be quick to re-brand yourself. (But not too often.) Fortunately, people's memories are fairly short. Accentuate the change by altering your behaviours, changing the people around you. It helps if you can associate your re-branding with other changes such as a promotion or an office move.

How to manage your career path

Career path management is essential to success. You can't rely on fate to get you where you want to go.

Set clear goals for what you want to achieve in your career. The aim is success, so go for what you are most likely to succeed at, not what you wish you could be good at.

What do I want
from my career?

Take the initiative – only by taking action will opportunities to reach your goal present themselves. In general, it is better to choose jobs that provide skills and experience, rather than money or prestige – these may be your ultimate goals, but a small gain now may hold you back from much greater success in the future. As soon as you stop learning – move on. You must keep actively moving towards your goal.

Go for your biggest development needs first. Don't get distracted by other concerns. It is very easy to pursue too many goals at the same time and achieve none of them.

Make sure every job you do teaches you something valuable.

A mentor is a valuable aid to success. Find someone with wisdom and experience that you can trust to provide you with a clear perspective, provide support and give you courage. In some cases a mentor may be able to actively help you achieve your goals. If nothing else, it helps to have someone to talk with to help order your thoughts. No matter how senior you are, a mentor is a powerful resource to have on your side.

Summary of main points

- The best way to play organizational politics is to brand yourself as a straight-shooter, make plenty of friends and work on getting tangible results.

- Play to your strengths and avoid projects that you are unlikely to succeed with easily.

- Every job should help you get closer to your career goals.

19 How to Become a Great Manager

What makes a great manager?

We want to believe we are great at what we do. But how can we tell?

For what it's worth, here is a formula for greatness (in just about anything):

- master the technical skills;

- demonstrate success;

- be an inspiration to others; and

- leave your mark.

In this chapter we are concerned with developing mastery of management in a systematic way. For if you do that, other things will surely follow:

- success will come with mastery; and

- a professional attitude to management is sure to set a powerful example in a world where management development is still shockingly ad hoc.

It is up to you to find a way to leave your mark.

> ### Smart people to have on your side: Jack Welch – former chairman and CEO of GE
>
> In recent times, few managers have been as exalted as GE's Jack Welch. During his 20 years as Chairman and CEO of GE, the company's market value has increased from $13 billion to over $400 billion.
>
> Jack Welch's ability as a manager is rooted in basic management skills – a passionate interest in cultivating people, an ability to delegate to competent deputies, and a real interest in how his businesses work. He also attributes his success to a great energy that stems from his passion for business.
>
> Welch has also brought many of the new management-guru ideas to GE: quality management, empowerment, organizational flexibility and change-management skills. GE's quality management programme in particular is a model for other companies.

In this chapter we'll look at some of the key interpersonal and self-management skills you'll need to master:

- delegation;

- dealing with employee disputes;

- seeing the big picture and detail together;

- organizing yourself; and

- managing your attitude.

And because leadership is an increasingly important skill for managers, we'll have a closer look at how to lead people.

In the next chapter, Chapter 20, 'How to Teach Yourself New Skills', we'll look at how to go about developing these skills.

How to master management

Critical management skill: delegation

The single most important skill in management is delegation. Succeed at delegation and you are well on your way to mastering management.

Learn how to set the right goals for people, keep track of their progress and problems, and provide them with the right kind of support. Too many managers set their employees up for failure. Masterful managers set their employees up to succeed.

Only through effective delegation can a manager make the most of the skills of their most valuable resource: their staff. We've already seen the theory (Chapter 10, 'How to Delegate'), but managers also need to adapt their management style to the needs of individual employees.

Unfortunately, there's no recipe for tapping human potential – everyone is different. The best you can do is to try to understand people better. How are they similar and how are they different? What motivates them? What are their needs? What are their abilities? What are their preferences? What are their comfort zones? What do they fear? What are their weaknesses? What are their conflicts of interest? Are they telling me everything?

So are managers really expected to become psychology experts? Yes! But you don't need to rush out and buy any books, or take a university course. Most importantly, you need to develop your ability to listen to and observe people and try to understand what they are thinking. *Then* you can help them to contribute in the best way they can.

Mentoring provides many benefits for both mentor and mentee. Not least of the benefits for mentors is the chance to see how others think, and learn what motivates them. And acting as a mentor also helps your employees to trust you – an essential part of delegation.

Critical management skill: dealing with employee disputes

For most managers, dealing with interpersonal disputes is one of the most difficult and frustrating aspects of their job.

Managers can set rules to help reduce such conflicts. A guiding principle should be that negative personal feelings and behaviours do not belong in the workplace.

A strong goal-oriented management style can often reduce conflict. It gives people an incentive to cooperate to achieve their goals. And it brings people closer as they share in collective victories. Conflicts are much more likely when people have conflicting interests.

But personality clashes are nevertheless inevitable and solutions are necessary. Most conflicts are caused by mutual misunderstandings, so often it is enough for people to talk through their issues with each other. If that fails, a more radical intervention may be needed. The manager must act as a fair and impartial judge and rely only on verifiable facts. A clear, effective solution must be arrived at quickly so that the group can get back to productive work.

Critical management skill: seeing the big picture and little picture at the same time

Managers face a tricky task. Success in business is often in the details. But the complexity of the organization makes it impossible to keep track of everything. Abstractions provide a way to see the broader patterns. But you need to see the big picture and the little picture at the same time.

See the big picture in the details; and see the details of implementation in the grand vision.

Too abstract? When we discussed core competence, we saw that maintaining a pure big-picture view can lead you into trouble because managers often over-generalize the nature of their company's core competencies e.g. 'efficient manufacture of small-value items'. Instead, you need to also be able to keep your eye on what is happening on the factory floor – what that actually means in terms of the actions, skills and decisions made by the operating employees. Core competence is a valuable big picture idea, but to work, the detail must also be kept in mind.

So learn the big picture ideas in this book and learn to see them at work in your business. But also get out on the factory floor; meet people face to face; ask questions; encourage people to tell you what's on their mind. And learn to think about both at the same time.

Critical management skill: organize yourself

We looked at various techniques for time efficiency in Chapter 9, 'How to Manage'. Your time is your most valuable resource – so use it well. Especially, try to become a master of prevention rather than cure.

To that end, it is worth trying to keep yourself organized. Managers have to juggle so many things at once that they can't possibly cope without a decent system for keeping track. Develop a system that works for you. And stick to it.

Smart quotes

'Very few managers use their time as effectively as they could. They think they're attending to pressing matters, but they're really just spinning their wheels.'

Bruch and Ghoshal, 'Beware the Busy Manager' (*HBR*, Feb 2002)

Critical management skill: managing your attitude

Many managers find that their biggest problems have little to do with the skills required to do their jobs and far more to do with their ability to manage themselves. Stress, busywork and lack of time seem to be the biggest complaints of any manager.

There is a range of common symptoms:

- stress – due to lack of time and overwork; general feelings of anxiety or dread;

- frustration – leading to cynicism and apathy despite initially high expectations;

- agitation – feeling a constant and urgent need for immediate action;

- procrastination – putting important things aside, often with a sense of fear when contemplating them; and

- emptiness – a feeling of uncertainty about whether your job is worthwhile.

These symptoms are part of a self-reinforcing cycle and they are shockingly common amongst managers. They happen because of the way we all respond to stressful situations. But however natural, they are nevertheless unproductive.

Fortunately there is a way to break the cycle:

- set a few big/important goals to achieve in your job;

- use these goals to drive you;

- find ways to avoid or offload small, less important tasks and distractions;

- set aside time each day for doing important tasks and plan in advance how you will use these periods;

- find ways to take control of your situation, rather than be at the mercy of others to achieve your goals. For example, take control of dysfunctional interactions with your boss to ensure you can be effective; and

- give yourself some much needed down-time.

By goal setting, focusing on what matters and taking control, you reduce stress, achieve more, save energy for attacking the big problems and stay positive. The results can only be good.

Smart quotes

'One reason that purposeful managers are so effective is that they are adept at husbanding energy.'

Heike Bruch and Sumantra Ghoshal, 'Beware the Busy Manager'
(*HBR*, Feb 2002)

Learn how to lead

You'll notice that the word 'leadership' has crept into this chapter. What happened to the stereotype of managers as dull bureaucrats shuffling memos back and forth all day?

These days, managers are expected to be leaders too: as if we should all become business Napoleons. Can you imagine a company full of inspirational leaders? All egos and orders and no action!

But that's not exactly what we mean by leadership in business.

We have already noted the trend towards greater autonomy and responsibility amongst employees. One of its consequences is that more people are being asked to demonstrate leadership in their jobs. For managers it means new skills to learn.

Most people assume that leadership is a personality trait – you are either a born leader or you aren't. Fortunately for most of us, it is simply not true. Yes, there are some people who seem to exude charisma – people who could lead a polar bear through the Sahara desert. But

Smart quotes

'Management is about coping with *complexity*; leadership is about learning how to cope with rapid *change*:

- Management involves planning and budgeting; leadership involves setting direction.
- Management involves organizing and staffing; leadership involves aligning people.
- Management provides control and solves problems; leadership provides motivation.'

John Kotter, 'What Leaders Really Do' (*HBR* 1990)

the good news is that you can be a highly effective leader without such rare qualities. This is lucky, because in the new business environment almost everyone is expected to lead and there just aren't enough Napoleons to go around.

Smart quotes

'The most pernicious half-truth about leadership is that it's just a matter of charisma and vision – you either have it or you don't. The fact of the matter is that leadership skills are not innate. They can be acquired and honed.'

John Kotter, 'What Leaders Really Do' (*HBR*, 1990)

Smart quotes

'A leader has willing followers-allies: followers are the underlying element that defines all leaders in all situations. Leadership occurs as an event: as discrete leader-follower interactions in specific circumstances.'

Warren Blank, *The 9 Natural Laws of Leadership*

What do you have to do to be an effective leader?

The critical feature of leadership is not the leader but the followers!

The primary concern of a leader is not how to be leaderly, but how to meet the four needs of their followers: mission, trust, strategy and organization (see box).

But there are many ways to fulfil these needs. So long as you satisfy all four needs, you can lead effectively. You have a lot of choices as to how you satisfy these needs – your personality and the nature of the leadership task will determine what will work best for you in a given situation.

Smart quotes

'"Leadership personality", "leadership style" and "leadership traits" do not exist. Among the most effective leaders I have encountered, some locked themselves into their office and others were ultra gregarious. Some were "nice guys" and others were stern disciplinarians. Some were quick and impulsive; others studied and studied again then took forever to come to a decision. Some were warm and instantly *simpatico*; others remained aloof. Some spoke of their family; others never mentioned anything but the task in hand. Some leaders were excruciatingly vain; some were self-effacing to a fault. Some were austere in their private lives; others were ostentatious and pleasure loving. Some were good listeners, but among the most effective were also a few loners who listened only to their inner voice.'

Peter Drucker

Leadership need: provide a clear uniting mission

Followers look to their leaders primarily to help them achieve something they all want. The leader's first job is therefore to unite people behind a single common mission.

In business, followers are not often all that highly motivated. Great leaders manage to generate passion for their mission. It helps to have a worthy cause (e.g. making life better for customers). But leaders must communicate why their mission matters, whatever it may be.

> **Smart quotes**
>
> 'Leaders have the enduring task of inspiring and motivating people to put aside small differences in the interests of larger causes.'
>
> Rosabeth Moss Kanter, 'Lasting Leadership Lessons' (Article)

A leader's mood can have a strong effect on the mood of the followers. Some leaders create a tangible buzz of excitement. But for the rest of us, it helps to show 'optimistic conviction'. Optimism helps followers maintain a positive attitude. Conviction communicates determination, task-focus and commitment.

Leadership need: earn trust and respect

People will only submit to being a follower if they trust their leader.

But followers aren't going to hand over authority and power to just anyone. A leader is going to have to earn the trust and respect of followers first and convince them the mission can be achieved. Some leaders demonstrate that they have the necessary skills or experience. Others earn respect through the strength of their commitment to the task. And yes, some leaders command loyalty through force of personality and charisma alone.

Smart quotes

'Followers will give their hearts and souls to authority figures who say, "you really matter". Followers want a feeling of community. Followers want excitement, challenge and edge in their lives.'

Robert Goffee and Gareth Jones, 'Followership: It's personal, too' (*HBR*, Dec 2001)

If trust is going to be maintained, the leader needs to show respect for people, their ideas and their needs. It helps to be open and honest. A clear commitment to the task is also likely to help.

Trust is a fragile thing. It is strong in victory and weak in failure. Leaders should go for quick momentum-creating wins to strengthen the followers' trust.

Leadership need: choose the right strategy

Clearly, the mission isn't going to be accomplished unless the right choices get made.

So, a primary task of leadership is to provide the group with an effective way to make good decisions. Of course, the easiest approach is for the leader to make *all* the important decisions. Decision-making ability is often the primary reason followers choose a particular leader.

A leader is responsible for ensuring that the group makes the right decisions.

But it isn't necessary, nor indeed always advisable, for the leader to make decisions alone. The more people feel a part of the decision-making process, the more trust they have in the leadership process and the more ownership they have of the mission.

So the leader can coordinate a group decision-making process instead – setting and enforcing rules to help the *group* come to effective decisions.

Leadership need: organization – let everyone contribute

Effective organization is also needed if the group is to get things done. Many different approaches can succeed: hands-on management of detail, or deferring to others; creating a hierarchy of duties or setting broad goals.

Just as important is to ensure that everyone can contribute. People are happy to put in a lot of effort for what they believe in, so long as their effort is valued. But anxious followers are likely to become cynical and disillusioned if they are unable to contribute effectively.

Followers need to know:

● What do I need to do?

● How will it contribute?

● Who do I turn to if I have any problems?

An effective organization answers these questions.

Summary of main points

● Managers looking to master their profession should take time to develop their interpersonal and self-management skills.

● Increasingly, managers are expected to effect real change on their organizations. As a result, leadership is becoming a critical management skill. There are many approaches to leadership, which needn't be grand or charismatic to be effective, so long as four key needs are met: mission, trust, strategy and organization..

20 How to Teach Yourself New Skills

Learn to learn

Business makes for an interesting career because it requires so many different skills, each requiring a different style of learning. The approaches discussed in this chapter will improve your ability to learn and also help you to develop your employees. This chapter will teach you how to learn.

> Before you can learn, you must learn to learn.

Technical subjects require an academic approach to learning. For subjects such as accounting and finance there is no substitute for hitting the books. Careful study of the concepts, rules and procedures are necessary. This is exactly the kind of learning you are familiar with from school. Colleges or business schools, which specialize in technical training, are worth considering if these are the skills you need to develop.

Some skills rely on big-picture concepts: strategy especially, but also marketing and management. These change the way you think about problems. They require careful thought, imagination and practice before they can be applied effectively to real-world business problems. Keep a big-picture idea in mind as you work and you'll start to see how it relates to your business.

Many businessmen have an intuition for what will work in their industry. They learn to see familiar patterns and know intuitively what they mean. There is really no substitute for experience in developing these skills. But you can accelerate your learning by consciously reviewing your experiences. Take the time to ask yourself what went well and what went badly, how well your expectations matched what happened and which of your beliefs were demonstrated or contradicted. Create hypotheses and see if they are confirmed or refuted by experience.

Management also requires many skills that depend on the manager's *behaviour*. For example, many people reflexively get frustrated and angry when presented with problems – a reaction that is hardly encouraging for an already fearful and embarrassed employee looking for help. Changing behaviours is probably one of the toughest challenges. Even when we know we want to behave in a different way, it can be painfully difficult to actually make the change.

How to read a book

Obviously, if you've made it to Chapter 20, you can read a book. But there are in fact many ways to get information from books. The style of the *Smart Things to Know about …* series offers many different ways to get information. You can read this book from cover to cover and ponder every word, or read it quickly and take in as much as you can. Or you can skim through it using the titles and captions to get an idea of the big concepts, reading more deeply on topics that catch your eye. Or you can just pick one chapter to read because it relates to an issue that you've faced yourself.

'Learning without thought is labour lost.'

Confucius

But the way to get the most from a book is to re-think the ideas yourself. What do your experiences tell you? What else have you read on the subject? How does your experience fit in with the ideas in this book? What can you add? What do you agree with and disagree with? How does your approach differ from what's presented in the book? Only when you know you could write a better book can you be sure you've got everything it has to offer.

The ideas in this book are a starting point – disagree with them, refine them and improve on them. Feel free to scribble your notes in the margins. When you can do this, it will truly become your book.

How to change your behaviour

Don't try to change your behaviour if you can possibly avoid it! It's a really hard process and takes a lot of time and patience. There are no short cuts and your mind and body can be horribly stubborn.

One area where business people most often look to change their behaviour is in presenting. Put the average Joe up in front of 200 of their peers and what happens? Nervousness, lots of 'ums' and 'ahs', odd gestures, monotonous delivery and fidgeting. People pay lots of money to highly trained professionals to teach them better presenting behaviours. But you probably have many of the right behaviours already – we're all great presenters when we're sharing an idea with our friends – we have passion and confidence and we're engaging and clear. So use the behaviours you already know from one environment and take them to another. Use jokes, passion and eye-contact to make it feel like you're talking to friends

– and suddenly it all comes together. When they get into the habit, even some of the worst presenters can quickly become highly engaging. They may not become masterful orators (that really does take training), but they get the message across effectively, and that's what counts.

So if you can find a situation in which your instinctive behaviours are the ones you want, you'll save a lot of effort by translating them to the required setting. Parenting, family, friendships, sports teams, school etc. all provide environments in which to develop behaviours that will be useful in business.

Smart answers to tough questions

Q: How can you change your behaviour?

A:

- Know exactly what you want to change and why you *need* to change. Keep it simple and stick to one thing at a time. Make a public commitment to change.
- Analyse your past mistakes and situations in which the new behaviour was needed. Try to identify the causes of problems and eliminate them one by one.
- Get frequent 'perfect practice'. Use drills that accentuate the required behaviours. Create controlled situations in which you can practise the new behaviour. Start slowly, be thoughtful and careful, and slowly increase the speed, stress etc. until you are ready to try it for real. Be patient and don't rush yourself. Continue each session only as long as you can hold your concentration.
- Visualize yourself doing it correctly.
- Get in the habit of self-talk. Give yourself lots of positive feedback when you do the right thing, and be easy on your mistakes. Don't aim too high too soon.
- Get help. Even just someone to talk to about what you're going through. A good coach can make the task much easier. Keep a record of your progress.
- Keep going – you'll get there eventually!

What if you can't find a suitable response that's appropriate? How do you go about changing your behaviour? The method described below is a modified version of the change programme we saw in Chapter 15, 'How to Manage Change', and similar to the process professional athletes use.

Business isn't about being perfect; it's about achieving success. You can be successful if you're good at just one thing. Focus on your strengths and learn to recognize and avoid your weaknesses. It's just a lot easier.

How to use feedback to speed up learning

Feedback is essential to all kinds of learning.

> **Smart answers to tough questions**
>
> Q: How can you use feedback to aid learning?
>
> A: Feedback is essential in learning. There are four different kinds:
> - *Positive feedback*. You do something and as a consequence something happens to tell you that you did the right thing.
> - *Negative feedback*. You do something and something happens to tell you that you did the wrong thing.
> - *Incentives*. When you do something wrong (or right) it is associated with an unpleasant punishment (or pleasant reward).
> - *Confused or absent feedback*. You receive sometimes positive and sometimes negative signals about the behaviour or no signal at all.

The best way to learn is through frequent, immediate, positive feedback. Every time you do the right thing, you receive confirmation of this. Very quickly you get good at doing the right thing.

Negative feedback is often necessary – people need to know when they've done something wrong. But it can be disheartening to have to discover the right actions through trial and error alone. Negative feedback leads to learning, but more slowly than positive feedback. It works best when accompanied by a clear reminder of the correct behaviour.

The best way to use feedback to enhance your learning is as follows:

- Make sure you are aware of the correct/desired behaviour.

- Initially affirm efforts that are even slightly close to the desired behaviour and slowly narrow the criteria for what constitutes correct behaviour.

- Use negative feedback for obviously incorrect behaviours. Use it to remind yourself of the correct behaviours.

- Maintain feedback until the behaviour is deeply entrenched.

Punishment and reward provide incentives for behaviours, but tend to be poor tools for learning complex new behaviours. The incentive itself often becomes the focus of attention rather than the action being learned. When the behaviour is hard to do correctly, punishment and reward can lead to stress, frustration and anger. Incentives, when they are used, should be small to ensure focus remains on feedback.

Reward and punishment are best suited to coercing people to do things they are already capable of, rather than to encouraging learning.

Confused/absent feedback is a lack of useful feedback. If you are trying to learn new behaviours, ensure you know what constitutes correct behaviour so that you can provide frequent, useful feedback.

Many managers prefer not to give negative feedback to their subordinates, either because they find it difficult or patronising, or simply because they are inconsistent in their praise and temperamental in their mood.

Most managers give far too little feedback, giving instead large rewards and punishments a long time later e.g. at the end of a review period.

The result of both of these behaviours is poor learning. As learning becomes more important in business, managers need to learn to give their staff frequent feedback.

Tread your own path to learning

You can learn a lot from other people. But there is a real danger in trying to 'catch-up' to someone else's ability.

It's often very hard to copy someone else. They do things in a way that suits them, so you will probably have to work much harder to get the same results. And often you cannot see the most critical factors in their learning – their mental preparation and attitude, for example.

It's also best not to use other people to measure your progress against. You'll always be mentally pushing hard to catch up. The result is likely to be more stress, which actually reduces your ability to learn. Instead be motivated by improving on your past performances and you'll find you improve much faster.

When learning has a practical purpose that means something for you, it is likely to be much more relevant and motivating and you'll improve faster. If you want to be a doctor, you have a reason for learning endless Latin names for parts of the anatomy – a task that would drive anyone else mad.

The best way to learn is to teach

The best way to learn is to teach. The discipline of guiding someone else through a subject forces you to be very clear in your mind about it. In the process you can more easily uncover your own uncertainties and apply thought to ideas that you had taken for granted.

Those who can, do. Those who want to learn, teach.

It can help greatly to act as a mentor. Not only can you develop your mentee's skills, but you will also find you learn a great deal too.

Lifelong learning

Learning is for life. To be really good at anything takes a long time – most people only reach complete competence in a complex skill after 10 years of learning. It is impossible to separate your education from the rest of your life – learning is a continuous part of everything you do.

Smart quotes

'Great leaders want to learn every day. They never stop learning.'

Jeffrey Immelt, Incoming CEO of GE

I wish you great successes in business and I hope the ideas in this book help you achieve them!

Appendix

Where to find more information

The Smart People to Have on Your Side have helped us along the way in this book. They are here because their books and articles have been profoundly influential in shaping business thinking. Their books are excellent places to get more sage advice from these intellectual Titans. Not all of their books are worth the effort required to read them. Many of their ideas can be obtained more easily from short articles they've written or from books that summarise their ideas. In many cases their ideas have been highly influential, but their books have become out-dated. Some of their most useful books and articles are listed below.

Useful books and articles to read next

General business/compilations of business thought

Peter Drucker: *On the Profession of Management* (compilation: 1998) – the best of Drucker's *Harvard Business Review* essays.

Tom Peters and Robert Waterman: *In Search of Excellence* (1982) – the original popular management book featuring many management ideas that remain cutting-edge.

Tom Peters: *Thriving on Chaos,* (1987) – a holistic prescription for creating excellent companies that can adapt to change. (Watch out: it's written in a somewhat disconcerting format.)

Henry Mintzberg: *Mintzberg On Management* (compilation: 1989) – collected pragmatic advice on management.

Rosabeth Moss Kanter: *On the Frontiers of Management* (compilation: 1997) – a compilation of Moss Kanter's *HBR* articles over 15 years with the common theme of empowerment.

Carol Kennedy: *Guide to the Management Gurus* (1991) – slightly dated introduction to the most influential management thinkers.

Joseph Boyett and Jimmie Boyett: *The Guru Guide* (1998) – an idiosyncratic exploration of some of the most fashionable ideas in management today and the thinkers behind them.

The manager's role

Henry Mintzberg: 'The Manager's Job' (article: *HBR* Mar–Apr 1990) – debunking myths about managers' roles.

Heike Bruch and Sumantra Ghoshal: 'Beware the busy manager' (article: *HBR* Feb 2002) – why managers are frequently unproductive and what to do about it.

Marketing and selling

Philip Kotler: *Marketing Management* (first published in 1967 but frequently updated) – weighty and all-inclusive compendium of the ideas and practice of marketing. It is also a manifesto for Kotler's view that marketing is the defining role in business. Everything is in here … somewhere.

Production and efficiency

C.K. Prahalad and Gary Hamel: 'The Core Competence of the Corporation' (article: *HBR*, May–Jun 1990) – core competence explained.

Tony Bendell: 'The Quality Gurus' an excellent introduction to the quality management movement.
(website: 2002) (www.dti.gov.uk/mbp/bpgt/m9ja00001/9ja000011.html)

Innovation and creativity

Edward De Bono: *Serious Creativity* (1992) – compilation of De Bono's ideas and how to use them in business.

Rosabeth Moss Kanter: 'Creating the Culture for Innovation' (article: 2001) – how to prevent your organization from stifling innovation.

Strategy and planning

Michael Porter: *On Competition* (compilation: 1998) a collection of articles on competition and strategy.

Henry Mintzberg: 'Crafting Strategy' (rticle: *HBR* Jul-Aug 1987) – how strategy really gets made.

Organization and teams

Henry Mintzberg: 'Organization Design: Fashion or Fit?' (article: *HBR*, Jan–Feb 1981) – the five organizational forms and when to use them.

Jon R. Katzenbach and Douglas K. Smith: 'The Discipline of Teams' (article: *HBR* Mar–Apr 1993) – when to create teams and how to make them work.

Change management

John Kotter: 'Leading Change' (article: *HBR*, Mar–Apr 1995) – the eight stages and pitfalls of change programmes.

Rosabeth Moss Kanter: *When Giants Learn to Dance* (1989) – how to get small company flexibility from big companies.

Leadership

John Kotter: 'What Leaders Really Do' (article: *HBR* Dec 2001) – how leadership differs from management and how to develop both sets of skills.

Rosabeth Moss Kanter: 'Lasting Leadership Lessons' (article: 2001) – a very brief summary of Moss Kanter's thoughts on leadership.

Robert Gofee and Gareth Jones: 'Followership: It's Personal Too' (article: *HBR* Dec 2001) – a brief essay on how to win the hearts of followers.

The future of business/careers

Peter Drucker: *Management Challenges for the 21st Century* (1999) – Drucker's vision of management in the next century, mainly based on trends already taking place.

If you enjoyed this book, you'll be happy to know that there are now *Smart Things to Know about …* books on practically every area of business. They are an ideal way to delve deeper and quickly discover the most important ideas on a subject. Other titles in this series are listed on the front page of this book.

Internet resources

Finally, you might also find the following Internet resources useful in furthering your business knowledge.

Academic business journals and articles

www.hbsp.harvard.edu/hbr/ – *Harvard Business Review.*

www.mckinseyquarterly.com – *McKinsey Quarterly.*

Business schools and executive education

www.businessweek.com/bschools/ – *Business Week*'s news and reviews of business schools.

www.bschool.com – website dedicated to compiling information on business schools.

www.business.com/directory/management/education_and_training/ – for more links to management education sites.

General business resources

www.executivelibrary.com – wide array of business-related Internet links.

www.business.com – search engine for business related content.

www.fastcompany.com – magazine style content focusing on business.

Index